PR
TRANSFC
ED

During this unprecedented moment in higher education, this book engages the idea of transformative innovation, applying it to higher education through a series of key insights, each designed to equip educators as they seek to design an education that prepares our young people for the future. It is a deeply relevant and eminently practical resource.

—John J. DeGioia
President of Georgetown University

Transforming Higher Education is a call to action for educators to rethink their futures. Bill Sharpe and Graham Leicester have given us a toolbox filled with proven methods for institutional change. I, like many others in education who lead transformative innovation initiatives, have long felt the need for a book that dealt in a straightforward way with the specialized problems and challenges facing schools, colleges, and universities. The authors' compelling descriptions of future scenarios and their careful depiction of the three horizons that seem to rush at all planners with increasing speed are filled with practical advice about how to engage educators and rise above the common pitfalls of transforming academic enterprises. Their methods ring true. These tools will be welcomed by leaders and will quickly become part of a new design vocabulary for this important sector.

—Professor Richard DeMillo
Executive Director of the 21st Century Universities
at the Georgia Institute of Technology

Transforming Higher Education provides a road map for innovative change in our educational systems that is both compelling and pragmatic. It not only will help readers to envision an educational future that is not simply reactive to current pressures and challenges, but it will allow them to identify new paths for radical change and improvement that address their own specific educational needs, as well as those of society.

—Robert S. Feldman
Professor of Psychological and Brain Sciences,
Senior Advisor to the Chancellor,
University of Massachusetts Amherst

The Three Horizons framework is an incredibly useful approach to strategy development in the university environment. It requires both "visionaries" and "managers" to engage in open dialogue about the magnitude and pace of change so that they can invest in the appropriate innovations for the institution.

The Three Horizons framework is something that is very suitable for the academy. The notion of multiple horizons existing simultaneously creates an opportunity for accommodation of multiple perspectives and constructive dialogue regarding critical decisions a campus must make. Getting people out of entrenched positions—by forcing them to consider multiple realities—will be essential to making real progress.

Transforming Higher Education provides a provocative view on how higher education could shift over the next decade, not by looking in a crystal ball, but by evaluating changes that are already in place. Colleges and universities should review these scenarios and ask themselves if they are really prepared for what the future may hold.

—Jeff Denneen
Partner, Bain & Company

Graham and Bill provide a thought-provoking examination of how technology and other disruptive factors are transforming higher education. But more importantly, they show how leaders can get in front of this change with their Three Horizons methodology and ultimately create a new model where educators and students can all succeed.

—Peter Cohen
President, University of Phoenix

TRANSFORMING
HIGHER
EDUCATION

Who Will Create the Future?

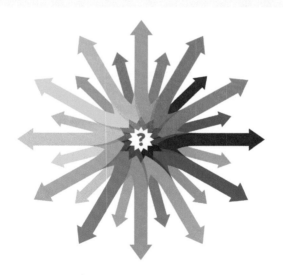

Graham Leicester & Bill Sharpe

NEW YORK   CHICAGO   SAN FRANCISCO   ATHENS
LONDON   MADRID   MEXICO CITY   MILAN
NEW DELHI   SINGAPORE   SYDNEY   TORONTO

1 2 3 4 5 6 7 8 9   LHN   23 22 21 20 19 18

ISBN   978-1-260-12184-1
MHID   1-260-12184-4

e-ISBN   978-1-260-12185-8
e-MHID   1-260-12185-2

This publication is designed to provide accurate and authoritative information in regard to the subject matter covered. It is sold with the understanding that neither the author nor the publisher is engaged in rendering legal, accounting, securities trading, or other professional services. If legal advice or other expert assistance is required, the services of a competent professional person should be sought.

> —*From a Declaration of Principles Jointly Adopted*
> *by a Committee of the American Bar Association*
> *and a Committee of Publishers and Associations*

Library of Congress Cataloging-in-Publication Data

Names: Leicester, Graham, author.
Title: Transforming higher education : who will create the future? / by Graham Leicester and Bill Sharpe.
Description: New York : McGraw-Hill, [2018]
Identifiers: LCCN 2017051241| ISBN 9781260121841 (acid-free paper) | ISBN 1260121844 (acid-free paper)
Subjects: LCSH: Education, Higher—United States—Planning. | Education, Higher—Aims and objectives—United States. | Educational technology—United States.
Classification: LCC LB2341 .L29 2018 | DDC 378.73—dc23
LC record available at https://lccn.loc.gov/2017051241

CONTENTS

ACKNOWLEDGMENTS

We are pleased to acknowledge a number of people whose work has made this book possible. The McGraw-Hill team and their partners helped us understand how the Three Horizons framework and scenarios can usefully help to illuminate changes in the world of higher education in the United States. In particular, we are grateful for the energy and commitment David Levin brought to this project and indebted to Catherine Mathis, Stephen Laster, Richard Keaveny, Rich DeMillo, and Anne Kirschner for all they did to shape the ideas in the manuscript. This work was only possible because of the initial scenario project undertaken by McGraw-Hill with Normann Partners. We also acknowledge our colleagues in IFF, in particular Denis Stewart, Val Corry, Graham Norris, and Frank Crawford for their work on K-12 education and Anthony Hodgson for his insights into dilemma thinking.

INTRODUCTION

SHIFT HAPPENS

It is now over 10 years since Karl Fisch, a high school teacher in Colorado, pulled together a set of data about the way the world is changing as a conversation starter for a staff faculty meeting. He called his presentation "Did You Know—Shift Happens." The presentation displayed a series of facts about the pace of change and the tectonic shifts in the world that are challenging many of our assumptions about the effectiveness of our education systems.

Fisch posted the presentation on his blog, the *Fischbowl*. It hit a nerve and quickly gained worldwide attention. It has been adapted, repurposed, updated, and variously republished ever since, in countless forms embracing all levels of education.

Why? Because it is a compelling and simple representation of what we all know but find difficult to face. We live in powerful times. The world is changing. The future is radically uncertain. And the challenge for educators is daunting. As the presentation memorably puts it: "We are currently preparing students for jobs that don't yet exist, using technologies that have not been invented, in order to solve problems we don't even know are problems yet."

BUT NOT IN EDUCATION

It is one thing to name the challenge, quite another to respond to it effectively. The Organisation for Economic Co-operation and Development (OECD) as long ago as 2002 described an era of "discontinuous change" in learning and education, "revolution, not reform." It is taking a long time to manifest as such.

In spite of its upbeat title, McKinsey's 2010 report "How the World's Most Improved School Systems Keep Getting Better" told a typically sorry tale about education reform overall. "Lots of energy, little light" was the headline summary. The report resolutely focused on "the few rays of hope that penetrate this bleak landscape." But overall the researchers found that in spite of significant investment over many years, performance remained flat. "Most OECD countries doubled or even tripled their spending on education in real terms between 1970 and 1994," they reported. "Unfortunately, student outcomes in a large number of systems either stagnated or regressed."[1] Certainly that is true of the United States where the Cato Institute has continued to produce regular updates on federal education spending tracked against test results, which confirm that this pattern continues.

Professor Richard DeMillo observes an equally familiar pattern with respect to higher education in his 2015 book *Revolution in Higher Education*.[2] He details a history of warn-

---

1 "How the World's Most Improved School Systems Keep Getting Better," Mona Mourshed, Chinezi Chijioke, and Michael Barber, McKinsey and Company (2010).

2 *Revolution in Higher Education: How a Small Band of Innovators Will Make College Accessible and Affordable*, Richard A. DeMillo, MIT Press (2015).

ings about the imminent collapse of the system dating back to beyond the 1880s. There is, he suggests, a repeating cycle of "calls for dramatic reform—quick and certain action to avoid sinking the entire system—followed by resistance to change." And the resistors have always been proved right: the system has always survived.

A WAVE OF CHANGE

But what if this time is different? DeMillo suggests that the optimistic narrative that "all downturns are temporary and best endured by appealing to the virtues of the academic endeavour" is no longer credible in the twenty-first century. He highlights the global economic crisis that started to manifest 10 years ago, plus the rapidly advancing forces of technology and digitization, as fundamental game-changers—for good or ill. Certainly, we can see how these trends, reinforced by the "creative destruction" of the market, are sweeping through education systems worldwide, and through higher education in particular.

In the United States we are already close to the point where every student will have both a suitable device to connect to the Internet and access to the connectivity to use it. The big tech companies are making huge plays in education, and a multitude of educational tech start-ups are soaking up investment—albeit largely focused at present on K-12. Machine learning, learning science, and big data are transforming student assessment, monitoring of faculty, performance incentives for individuals and institutions, and much else besides. The "Google generation" expects information to be free and education to be available at much lower prices, even as real costs mount. The seamless efficiency of a single-platform, cloud-based, all-around school learning performance assessment and administration system offering many of the benefits of present arrangements at a fraction of the cost is almost irresistible.

But we do have choices. The choice right now for higher education is the one outlined by the environmentalist Stewart Brand back in the 1970s. Once a new technology "rolls over you," he said, "if you're not part of the steamroller, you're part of the road."

CREATING THE FUTURE

This book is about being part of the steamroller—in other words, harnessing the power of this wave of technology and market-driven change to the deeper and more transformative aspirations of the sector.

It draws on two sources. The first is the authors' collective experience as members over many years of International Futures Forum (IFF), a group established in 2001 to explore how to take effective action in a complex world that we do not fully understand and cannot control. Given our interest in the future, and particularly in the twenty-first-century skills and competencies required to thrive in it, we have focused much of our work on education.[3] IFF itself is an educational charity.

What we have found is a clear recognition in the education system at all levels that the world is changing rapidly,

---

3 Graham Leicester is coauthor of a previous book published by Triarchy Press based on IFF's work with the K-12 sector: *Transformative Innovation in Education: A Playbook for Pragmatic Visionaries*, and also of a more wide-ranging study of twenty-first-century competencies (also from Triarchy Press): *Dancing at the Edge: Competence, Culture and Organization in the 21st Century*.

coupled with a real appetite to engage with that change. But at the same time, there is not much capacity to do so: teachers, faculty, and administrators have precious little time to think or to plan, training budgets are slim, there is no provision for facilitation or consultants' fees, and there is little spare capacity to introduce innovation in any event when the day job—keeping the plane in the air—is so demanding and financial pressures so high.

Our own approach therefore has been to work with the impulse for change *within* the system. We have seen throughout the system individuals and groups—some influential, some not—with a desire to harness the forces of change around them to realize their deeper aspirations for the sector, for their students, and for their professional selves. We call this kind of work "transformative innovation"—shifting the system toward a new pattern fit for the future and in tune with our longer-term aspirations rather than just fixing what's failing in the present. We have developed some simple tools and processes to support this practice in any setting: how to read the landscape of change, develop pathways through it, and then move into effective action.

Beyond this practical experience, the second source for this book is an immersion in the trends that are disrupting and potentially transforming higher education in the United States. No process can deliver without good content. So it is important to have a good grasp of the nature of the changes taking shape around us. We need to read the landscape in order to plot a pathway through it.

We are therefore particularly grateful for the generous access we have been granted to the recent McGraw-Hill Education (MHE) scenarios for higher education, published here for the first time. These form the substantive heart of the book. We welcome MHE's willingness to share this work with a wider audience. MHE is thinking seriously about how best to position itself in the current landscape. But it is not alone. This is something we all need to consider. MHE and its academic collaborators and conversationalists have given us all a step up in that process by sharing these scenarios. The core of the work is the research about trends and what we call "pockets of the future"—those instances of innovation in the present that point to disruption and change ahead. It goes without saying that decisions of interpretation and selection from this rich body of material are the authors' alone and should not therefore be taken as the view of MHE necessarily or of its customers and partners. Nor do we claim that our selection reflects MHE's own views. We have been fortunate to sample an extensive body of research.

These two approaches—a rootedness in practice plus an extensive and substantive examination of future trends—come together finally in the Appendix of the book. The Appendix provides a set of instructions for how to work with the content—captured in a deck of "futures cards" available as a complement to the book—to feed the difficult conversations about values, vision, hopes, and fears that need to take place within the faculty, between the faculty and administrators, between institutions and policy makers, and indeed with the wider public. IFF also offers a network of support for those who wish to play their part in creating the future. Introducing the new in the presence of the old, shifting systems toward a viable future rather than simply fixing what is failing in the present, is a distinctive practice that needs dedicated support. We hope the success of this book and the resources in the Appendix will stimulate others to help develop for the sector this much-needed infrastructure for transformative innovation.

OUTLINE OF THE BOOK

The book consists of four chapters.

Chapter One: Three Horizons
How should we think about the future?

This chapter introduces the Three Horizons framework as a simple tool for engaging thoughtfully and purposefully with the future—in particular doing so in a way that acknowledges our own agency, our own capacity to create the future we aspire to rather than simply adapting to the future created by others. This chapter also introduces the concept of transformative innovation that flows from a Three Horizons view of the landscape. It describes how this relates to and is distinct from other forms of "sustaining" or "disruptive" innovation.

Chapter Two: Waves of Change
Where are we?

Chapter 2 provides a detailed examination of what lies ahead, the waves of change that are sweeping over us driven by technology and the market. Drawing on MHE's detailed research, this chapter identifies 12 powerful "predetermined" forces that will be both highly influential and highly predictable over the coming years and that must be reckoned with. It closes with three scenarios for the future, each seen from a unique perspective (inferred through the MHE research but not necessarily reflective of the actual position of any institution or company): "Renewal from Within" (from the perspective of the higher education institutions themselves), "Education Remix" (from the perspective of the educational technology entrepreneurs, and venture capitalists), and "Big Tech Platforms" (from the perspective of certain big tech players and with an eye on the evolution of major platforms and the technologies supporting them).

Chapter Three: From Insight to Action

How can we develop a pathway forward?

Here we consider how to work skillfully in this complex landscape of change. If we are to navigate it effectively, we must first be clear about what we want—and how the values that underpin our vision might find a place within a system currently dominated by other values. The chapter explores these "value tensions" and shows how to work with them not as choices but as dilemmas. It also explores the notion of a "creative integrity," the small core pattern that we need to hold these dilemmas and stand for a different future, and that we hope will grow in strength, scope, and structure over time. And we will need to become more comfortable in taking our first step, and subsequent ones, into the unknown of a different future. That requires a new approach to risk management: if this work does not feel risky, then we are not doing it right.

Chapter Four: Supporting Transformative Innovation

What is needed to support those on the journey?

The final chapter outlines the enabling conditions and support structures that those responsible for policy and strategy at all levels in the system can usefully put in place to facilitate the practice of transformative innovation in higher education. It is not our default practice, so there are few supports routinely available. But following some simple guidelines can make a huge difference to the prospects of success, and the chapter points to a variety of resources and sources of support.

....

True to our reading of a world in which people have little time to think and even less to turn strategic thought into wise action, this is a short and necessarily simple book. It almost certainly does not do justice to the complexity of its subject matter. However, especially with the accompanying futures cards and the detailed facilitation and other resources in the Appendix, we hope it will at least provide enough encouragement to those standing on the brink of transformative change to step forward and make a first move. Start the conversation. Find some kindred spirits. Take a first step in shifting the system in the direction of your Third Horizon aspirations. We see the book and the facilitation instructions and resources in the Appendix as a way of making a very complex discussion more accessible—and indeed initiating it in a constructive way.

Making a difference in the face of all that stands in the way of making a difference in higher education, as in other areas, relies ultimately on an ever-expanding network of experiments by passionate people rising to the challenge of transformative innovation. Welcome to that group.

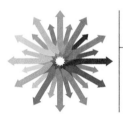

THREE HORIZONS

I n this first chapter we introduce the Three Horizons framework as a simple tool for ordering our thoughts about the future. Its great virtue is that it works with an intuitive grasp of how the future occurs to us: a landscape of uncertainty in which we too are actors. If we can become consciously aware of that intuitive appreciation, it is possible to work with the emerging future much more skillfully. In particular we can set about realizing our own aspirations in a fast-changing and complex world. This is the practice we call "transformative innovation."[1]

We start from the simple proposition that the future is unknown: it is characterized by *uncertainty*. Yet at the same time we are always *acting* toward the future, taking a step forward, moving in the direction of our longer-term aspirations.

---

1 See *Transformative Innovation: A Guide to Practice and Policy*, Graham Leicester, Triarchy Press (2016), and the extensive resources available at www.iffpraxis.com.

We do so by taking a view on the things that we expect to stay the same and that we can rely on and also on the things that we want to change. We are playing in a landscape that includes the known and the unknown, and we too, through our own actions, have a say in how the future turns out. We have *agency*.

These two features of uncertainty and agency combine to define the strategic landscape we need to consider if we are to act with the future in mind. It is a landscape of greater or lesser complexity, depending on how much we can rely on and what is in flux, the number of agents seeking to effect change, and the intensity and effectiveness of their actions.

There is a wide variety of tools and processes to help us engage with this complex landscape more effectively. As Figure 1.1 shows, if we map these against the two variables of agency and uncertainty, we can see that different tools are

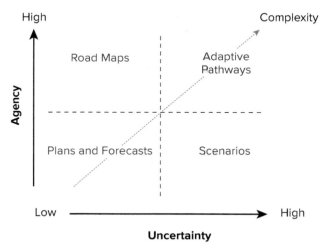

FIGURE 1.1 **Ways of thinking about the future.** Different tools are available, each suited to a different combination of agency and uncertainty in the operating environment.

designed for different parts of the landscape. Each assumes a different combination of the known and the unknown, and each makes different demands on our strategic capacity to move ourselves, our organizations, and the systems around us in the direction of our aspirations.

The area of low agency and low uncertainty is the domain of *plans and forecasts*. These tools are appropriate when you can usefully model the situation you are addressing based on past data, where the system in question is stable enough and known enough for knowledge of the past to be a good predictor of the near-term future. In those circumstances you can also expect a normal level of agency short of the heroic to be effective.

The area of high agency and low uncertainty is the domain of *road maps*. Typically road maps are used for setting a stretch goal and outlining steps and milestones along the way to achieving it. Follow the plan and the future will be as we desire it. This approach can be useful where organizations and actors can get together and pool purpose around a common aim, work out a route, and commit to following that path together.

That approach will work so long as the plan can legitimately tune out all uncertainty not considered relevant to the core pathway. Hence the technology industry can reliably roll out third-generation, fourth-generation, and fifth-generation mobile technology—so long as it does not need to take into account the myriad complex ways in which society worldwide is actually using it.

The area where it is uncertainty that is privileged rather than agency is the domain of *scenarios*. This is where the unknown and the uncertain take center stage. Scenarios are stories—about plausible futures that might come about given known trends, discontinuities, shocks to the system, and all kinds of interactions between them. The purpose of contemplating diverse scenarios is to shift organizations and actors into a mode where the future is acknowledged as uncertain. That way they are less likely to get stuck in a single view of the "official future" and be blindsided when the world changes around them. Unlike the road map, for example, the goal of scenario planning is not to reach a destination but to remain adaptable and agile, forewarned against surprises as the landscape changes—developing a capacity to read the pattern of change and to be better prepared for whatever it throws at us.

The fourth domain combines this acknowledgment of complexity and uncertainty in the operating environment with a high sense of agency, intention, and purpose. This is the domain of *adaptive pathways* where we are seeking not only to read the uncertain landscape but to shape it to our own ends. It is about creating the future we desire in the face of complexity. While equally goal-oriented, it differs from the road maps approach by acknowledging this complexity in all of its three dimensions:

1. **Dynamic complexity.** Everything connects to everything else, and the whole system is always in motion.

2. **Social complexity.** The system is also a human system characterized by a multitude of actors, worldviews, values, and so on.

3. **Generative complexity.** The system is fundamentally unpredictable and will naturally generate unintended or unanticipated consequences from any action.

In this adaptive pathways space, we hold a vision for the future and act in the moment. We allow the uncertainty to emerge, as the slope unfolds beneath our feet when we are skiing down a mountain, and resolve it through action moment by moment. This is not about following a road map. It is about maintaining a sense of direction and always taking the next step. The path is made by walking, and the only way to learn is to be in motion.

These domains and divisions are not impermeable. There are forms of scenario planning, for example, that pay greater attention to the aspirations and intentions, the agency, of the players involved. And emergent pathways can become so over-engineered as to become indistinguishable from road maps.

So another useful distinction between the different approaches described above involves considering the three factors we must always reckon with when thinking about the future: predetermined elements, critical uncertainties, and vision.

1. **Predetermined elements** are aspects of the future that, as the term suggests, we can confidently predict will occur. When heavy rains fall in the mountains, there are going to be consequences downstream. As Pierre Wack, one of the founders of scenario planning as a discipline, said: "This is not fortune telling or crystal-ball gazing. It is simply recognising the future implications of the rainfall that has already occurred." Likewise we can be reasonably confident in the field of higher education that, for example, bandwidth available in schools and colleges next year is on average going to be higher than it is this year. That is a pretty safe bet. The part of the future that is *known* in this way is critically important and often underplayed when we think of the future as a journey into the *unknown*. If we are to attain our aspirations for the future, then we will have to take the predetermined elements into account.

2. **Critical uncertainties** are elements or trends in the landscape that may have a significant impact on the future with which we are especially concerned. They are elements that we can discern, more or less clearly, in the present landscape that may play a critical role in the future depending on how they develop. They may go this way or that, occur or not. Typical examples include how society as a whole might respond to a changing world or how that response is reflected—or not—in government regulation. Will higher education institutions use greater bandwidth to enhance the classroom experience or to do away with classrooms altogether? We know after the rain that the floods are on the way. We cannot be certain how the wider system will respond.

3. **Vision** is an expression of the future we desire, the world we aspire to live in. Just like predetermined elements and critical uncertainties, vision contributes to the pattern of the landscape ahead. It does so through people holding that vision, putting in the necessary effort to work toward it, embodying it as far as possible in the present, and making a stand for it as a possible future.

Road maps, emphasizing agency and intention but downplaying uncertainty, will be dealing primarily with vision and predetermined elements. Scenario planning, downplaying agency and intention, will concentrate on predetermined elements and critical uncertainties. It is only in the adaptive pathways domain that we are thinking about all three factors—predetermineds, uncertainties, and vision.

This domain has come to be seen as the arena for *reflexive* futures thinking. It is reflexive in the sense that it recognizes we are both observers of an emerging future and actors influencing and creating it. This is the domain, in other words, of intentional transformation—the orientation that is explicitly explored in this book. It is in this domain that we have found Three Horizons to be a simple, intuitive, and highly effective framework.

THREE HORIZONS

Three Horizons gives us a way of working with the predetermineds and uncertainties involved in understanding the deeper processes of long-term societal change. Yet it also maintains a rootedness in practice—effective action that will help to shift any system toward our longer-term aspirations. IFF has used the model to frame discussion of intentional transformation over time in a variety of settings, e.g., energy policy, healthcare, financial services, criminal justice. And education.[2]

The core framework (see Figure 1.2) at first looks straightforward and familiar. We know that in order to sustain growth a company needs to think in terms of Three Horizons of the short, medium, and longer term: managing for current performance while also exploring future opportunities.[3] But it turns out that this simple model takes on some interesting and different characteristics when applied to patterns of social change and particularly change that is intentionally transformative.

---

2 For more information about the Three Horizons framework, visit www.iffpraxis.com/three-horizons.

3 This is the insight first described by three McKinsey consultants in *The Alchemy of Growth: Practical Insights for Building the Enduring Enterprise*, Mehrdad Baghai, Stephen Coley, and David White, Basic Books (1999).

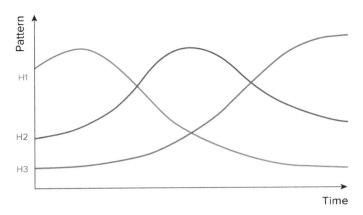

Pattern

H1

H2

H3

Time

FIGURE 1.2 **The Three Horizons framework.** A business-as-usual H1 pattern gives way over time to a new pattern in H3 better suited to the changed world, enabled by innovation in H2.

If we see the Three Horizons not as future time horizons but as three qualities of the future in the present, then the framework becomes reflexive. Each Horizon represents some playing out of a particular perspective on the future potential of the present moment, as experienced by an individual or a group.

These different perspectives occur quite naturally in any conversation about the future. After a while it is possible to tune in to three distinct "voices," the voices in effect of the Three Horizons: the voice of the manager wanting to keep things going, of the entrepreneur wanting to try something new, and of the visionary dreaming of a different world. So long as those different views are held as fixed mindsets, the dialogue between them does not go very well. But if they are held more lightly, as three equally legitimate *perspectives*, the dialogue can become generative and hopeful.

When appreciated in this way, as a tool for the practice of reflexive futures, Three Horizons has proved particularly useful for organizations and institutions navigating a complex and uncertain landscape, committed to a values-based vision of the future, but up against powerful forces (often including the market) that have a different future in mind. Often those forces are committed to reinforcing or improving existing systems, which continue to serve their interests well. A transformative vision of the future must be realized by working against the grain of this dominant culture. Three Horizons provides a natural framework for mapping this complex landscape, locating ourselves and others within it, and designing the kinds of initiatives that might be successful in shifting the system in the direction of our aspirations—practical hope through wise initiative.

The framework is very simply described (see Figure 1.2). It is framed by axes of "pattern" and "time." Pattern is a more general word for system: the vertical axis thus refers to the scale and the scope of the patterns that shape our lives in the domain of interest for our inquiry.

The First Horizon, H1

H1 is the dominant system at present. It represents "business as usual." We rely on these systems being stable and reliable. But as the world changes, so aspects of business as usual begin to feel out of place or no longer fit for purpose. Eventually business as usual will always be superseded by new ways of doing things.

The Third Horizon, H3

H3 emerges as the long-term successor to business as usual. It grows from fringe activity in the present, responses to failings in the H1 system that introduce completely new ways of doing things, but that turn out to fit the world that is emerging much better than the dominant H1 systems under strain.

The Second Horizon, H2

H2 is a pattern of transition activities and innovations, people investing in different responses to the ways in which the landscape changes, placing bets, making choices. Some of these innovations will be absorbed into the H1 systems to prolong their life; we call them "H2 minus" (H2–). Others will pave the way for the emergence of radically different H3 systems; these we call "H2 plus" (H2+).

....

We typically introduce the Horizons, and think about the way the dynamics change between them over time, in the order H1, H3, H2. Without a Third Horizon it is not possible to make a distinction between "defensive" or "sustaining" innovation (H2–) that makes existing systems better, cheaper, faster, more efficient, and so on and "transformative" innovation (H2+), which shifts the whole system fundamentally toward a different pattern more likely to be viable in the future. Anyone can disrupt a system, but you need to have a Third Horizon aspiration in view in order to disrupt it with a purpose.

As an example we might see H1 as the mainframe computer, H2 as the desktop, and H3 as mobile access to the cloud via the Internet. Or in terms of the school system, H1 might be universal mass education, H2 might be personalized education tailored to the student, and H3 might be open access education—what I want, when I want, where I want—possibly without traditional schools at all. The critical insight is that you cannot bring about an H3 system simply by improving H1.

As the framework with its three lines also suggests, all Three Horizons are always present. Aspects of H1—typically desirable features like safety and reliability—will persist in any new "business as usual." Aspects of H3 are always evident, if not obvious, in current discourse and argument and in all kinds of activity on the fringes of the dominant system. And H2, like a moving border between past and future, is all around us in examples of innovative alternative practice.

But the First Horizon's commitment is to survival. The dominant system can maintain its dominance even in a changing world either by crushing Second and Third Horizon innovation or by co-opting it to support the old system. Thus we might see quirky experimental programs at small liberal arts colleges taken up by bigger players to give them an air of radical chic, putting the smaller players out of business while toning down the original experience to render it "safe" for a wider market. Or professors reading their old lectures on YouTube—saving costs in the system but leaving the overall pattern fundamentally unchanged.

These behaviors lead to variants on the smooth transition depicted earlier. There is a "collapse and recovery" dynamic in which resources are poured into a failing H1 system against the grain of the universe until it eventually collapses (Figure 1.3). A new H3 pattern takes time to emerge through the wreckage. More common is the "capture and extension" scenario in which innovations in H2 are mainstreamed in order to prolong the life of the existing system against the grain of a changing world (Figure 1.4). And finally there is the more positive "overshoot" scenario in which investment pours into a promising pattern of innovation in H2 before it is ready to meet demand and when quality is variable (Figure 1.5). The bubble is followed by a bust, but H3 can grow strongly when confidence returns.

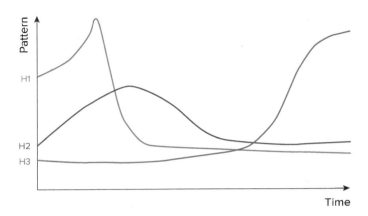

FIGURE 1.3 **Variant 1: Collapse and recovery.** Resources are sucked into an unsustainable First Horizon pattern that inevitably collapses. The Third Horizon pattern eventually comes through the wreckage.

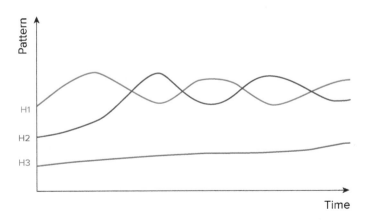

FIGURE 1.4 **Variant 2: Capture and extension.** Innovation in the Second Horizon is "captured" by the First Horizon to keep it going, starving the Third Horizon of resources and suppressing its emergence.

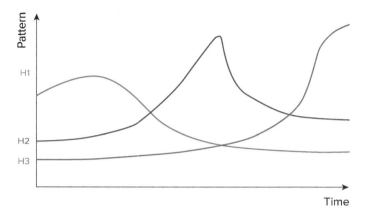

FIGURE 1.5 **Variant 3: H2 overshoot.** Investment pours into Second Horizon innovation before it is ready to bear the load—the tech bubble phenomenon. The Third Horizon eventually comes through strongly.

The framework offers a simple way into a conversation about:

- The dominant system and the challenges to its sustainability into the future, i.e., the case for change (Horizon 1).

- The desirable future state, the ideal system we desire and the already perceptible elements of it in the present that give us encouragement and inspiration (Horizon 3).

- The nature of the tensions and dilemmas between H3 vision and H1 reality, and the subtle processes of change, new ways of working, new capacities, new structures even, required to navigate the transition between them.

- The development of a mature perspective that accepts the need *both* to address the challenges to the First Horizon *and* nurture the seeds of the Third. This is not an either/or, good/bad discussion. We need both to "keep the lights on" today and to find a way of keeping them on in the future in very different circumstances.

Three Horizons: The Patterning of Hope[4] is the definitive guide to the framework and the surprising power in its simplicity. It identifies three central practices that Three Horizons encourages.

The first is to *see things as patterns*, to think systemically. The framework draws our attention toward systemic patterns rather than individual events or global trends. These patterns result from the activity and behavior of those who are participating in them and maintaining them in the present. Each Horizon in effect is developing a different quality already existing in the present, and which might become more prominent depending on how people choose to act—to maintain the familiar or pioneer the new.

That of course includes ourselves: we need to *put ourselves in the picture*. We are also actors and can choose which patterns we want to maintain and which we want to shift. The Third Horizon in the present is a pattern of activity pursued by people driven by their values, doing something they believe in.

Finally, it is possible to *convene the future* by listening for, and becoming adept at managing a conversation between, the voices of the Three Horizons described earlier. The voice of

---

4 *Three Horizons: The Patterning of Hope*, Bill Sharpe, Triarchy Press (2013).

Horizon One is the voice of the *manager*. It talks about maintaining the current system and usually expresses concern. The voice of Horizon Two is the voice of the *entrepreneur*. It talks about trying something different and often expresses a combination of urgency and frustration. The voice of Horizon Three is the voice of the *visionary*. It talks about dreams and deep aspirations and is usually both humble and inspiring.

These are three natural mindsets that will be revealed in any conversation about the future. Each of us can easily fall into any one of them depending on the subject under discussion. Yet it is also possible to adopt them lightly, not as mindsets but as perspectives on the situation. Figure 1.6 suggests how each position "hears" the other voices and the attitude each has to the other positions, both negative mindsets and positive perspectives. This is the critical reflexive turn. "Convening the future" means becoming aware of all these mindsets and perspectives, in each individual and in ourselves, and working with them to shift the conversation in a generative direction.

In the context of trying to find ways to stimulate new thinking throughout the higher education system, the Three Horizons framework's principal virtue is that people find it simple and intuitive. The three modes of thinking that it encourages—managing the existing system, brainstorming promising innovation, and aspiring to something better in the future—are perfectly natural and can be heard in any day-to-day conversation.

But in a professional environment, the voice of the Third Horizon is usually suppressed ("Dream on!"), the voice of the second is often dismissed ("That would never work here"), and the voice of the first is very rarely positive ("Let's face it: we're unlikely to come through this"). We tend to polarize into defendants of H1 and advocates for an "unrealistic"

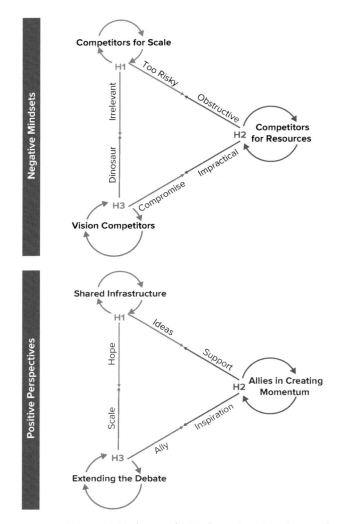

FIGURE 1.6 **How each Horizon typically views the others in negative and positive modes.** Each horizon typically has views on the other horizons (and on their fellows, e.g., H1 managers' views of other H1 managers, H3 visionaries' views of other visionaries). "Convening the future" involves encouraging all of these views to be expressed, inviting all these voices, both negative and positive, to join the conversation.

H3—without paying sufficient attention to the subtle processes in H2 that might enable the transition.

Part of the skill in facilitating the Three Horizons conversation lies in learning how to shift from the firmly held *mindsets* of the different Horizons to more loosely held, and usually more generative, *perspectives*. In practice, it is possible for all of us to imagine what the future might look like from the perspective of the manager, or the entrepreneur, or the visionary, and when we do so, we can have a more empathic and generative dialogue between us.

THREE FACES OF INNOVATION

A further dimension of the Three Horizons framework is the fresh insight it offers on the question of innovation.

Innovation in H1 is for efficiency. It is about improvement, getting the most out of the existing system, making it faster, cheaper, safer. This is typical of production processes, for example, or sports coaching: the "aggregation of marginal gains" in order to achieve excellence. In a changing world, it has variously been described as "maintaining," "sustaining," "defending," or "improving" innovation.

Innovation in H2 is about seeing and seizing opportunity. Different ideas are conceived, tried, and tested. Some work; others fail. But what is the selection mechanism? In practice, in the absence of any other frame of reference, innovations stand or fall in H2 depending on their capacity to support and appeal to H1. Business as usual, after all, holds most of the power and resources and takes the critical decisions about research funding, about purchasing, and about policy.

So, in practice, innovations in H2 have a tendency to look backward. Most of them are conceived in those terms—

designed to fix the existing system in H1. Others just happen to catch on—but again largely because they succeed in fixing or improving the old system, prolonging its life. Where something takes off at scale in business, it is usually because it has caught a mass market—the holy grail for much innovation. Likewise in policy circles, being taken up enthusiastically by the existing system is the unexamined goal of most would-be reformers.

But what if the goals of H1 are unsustainable? What if there is a growing sense that "we cannot go on like this" and that there is nothing much to be gained from doing the wrong thing faster? Innovation from an H3 perspective is about opening up a strategic conversation about the way the world is changing that allows us to reexamine the unstated assumptions of H1, including what constitutes "success" or "growth" or "excellence" or "value." H3 is the dimension in which we can talk seriously about Karl Fisch's "jobs that don't yet exist, using technologies that have not been invented, in order to solve problems we don't even know are problems yet." Without this H3 perspective all innovation in H2 is likely to be drawn toward improving the status quo.

With an active vision and imagination about the nature of the Third Horizon, we open up another possibility. We can design innovations that work to shift the existing system toward something radically different. Such innovations help create the conditions for the eventual realization of H3 aspirations. This is transformative innovation.

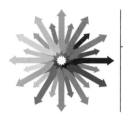

CHAPTER TWO

WAVES OF CHANGE

READING THE LANDSCAPE

I n 2014 the CEO of MHE, David Levin, instigated a strategic review of the future landscape for higher education. MHE was (and is) a major publisher of educational textbooks and so was seeing a rapid shift coming due to the arrival of artificial intelligence, digital curriculum, and widely available mobile broadband.

The review naturally also took into account equally dramatic signs that the landscape of higher education itself is under pressure to change: worrying levels of failure to complete degrees, concerns that graduates are not acquiring the skills for a competitive modern economy, waning performance of U.S. higher education in relation to other countries, online learning and do-it-yourself universities creating a "new ecosystem" in higher education, ongoing pressures for efficiency and value for money, concerns about narrow specialism squeezing out the broad liberal arts curriculum, and so on. All this in the context of the same wave of digital innovation disrupting MHE's core publishing business.

While a few elite, top-tier institutions are likely to have the reputation and the depth of resource to carry on much as they have done, evolving through and with these changes, for most others the landscape is both challenging and confusing in equal measure. Clayton Christensen, father of the concept of "disruptive innovation," remarked earlier in the decade and has repeated since that in the face of these waves of change, he anticipates as many as half of the 4,500 colleges and universities in the United States will fail within 10 years. So what are the astute strategic moves that will work with the grain of this landscape of change to ensure success or, better still, the realization of transformative potential?

For MHE the decline of traditional print media opened a pathway toward a future of harnessing artificial intelligence, digital content, and the potential of learning sciences to create a new range of learning products that would improve educational outcomes. At the same time those products could be designed to enhance the flow of data to students and faculty, allowing better decision making.

But this book is not about publishing. It is about the response of the institutions of higher education themselves to this same emerging landscape.[1] How might they too draw on the bedrock research and learning from the MHE strategic review process to determine an effective strategy of their

---

1 Colleges across the country are grappling with what their options are. There are some interesting approaches, including, for example, Georgia Tech's "Commission on Creating the Next in Education (CNE): What Will a Georgia Tech Education Look like in 2040" with extensive research on demographics, learner needs, pedagogy, and other drivers of change in higher education. See www.provost.gatech.edu/commission -creating-next-education.

own in the face of the predetermined elements and the critical uncertainties we can see in the landscape? More than that, drawing on the previous chapter, how might they incorporate their own vision and aspirations into the process, establishing pathways that promise not only survival but transformation—on their own terms?

THREE HORIZONS AND THREE SCENARIOS

The MHE process began with a Three Horizons mapping of the landscape of change:

- What are the concerns emerging within the dominant First Horizon pattern of higher education?

- What visions and aspirations are in play for radical improvement, and who is pursuing them?

- Where might we find evidence of their radical intent already in practice even at a small scale?

- What does the existing landscape of innovation look like—sustaining innovations designed to prolong the life of the existing system, disruptive innovations that look interesting but are yet to prove themselves at scale, and transformative innovations that promise a very different pattern of provision in the future?

The resulting Three Horizons map (Figure 2.1) highlights three critical dynamics: education system renewal, digital transition, and technology-enabled learning. These dynamics cannot be ignored: any institution of higher education at this stage in the twenty-first century must reckon with them.

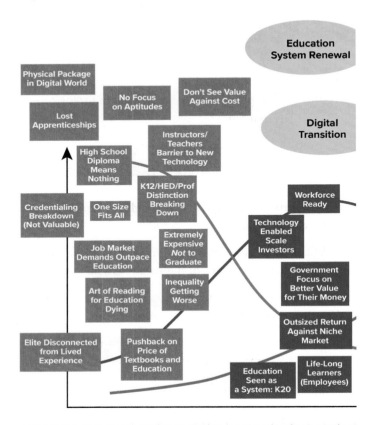

FIGURE 2.1 **The Three Horizons of higher education in the United States.** The results of an initial mapping of the landscape of change, including three critical dynamic drivers—the orange ovals. Red represents concerns with the dominant system at present. Green shows desirable features of a long-term successor. Blue represents the transitory landscape of innovation. (©2016, McGraw-Hill Education, Future of Higher Education)

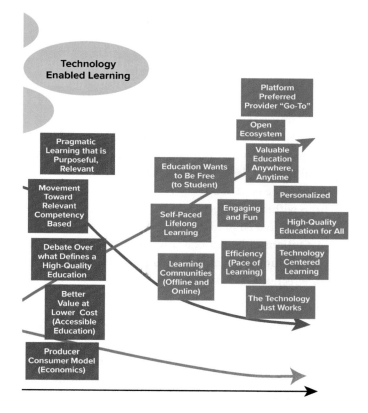

- **Education system renewal.** This captures an appreciation of ambiguity in the capacity of the higher education system to respond to its challenges, as they are showing up in the perceived failings of the current Horizon One system. Many of the problems now driving public discussion have been visible for a long time without being resolved, so there is widespread skepticism that they will be rapidly overcome. Yet the opportunity is there, and we can point to shining examples and promising innovations that suggest the system *does* have the capacity for renewal from within. Whether it does so successfully or not depends to a large extent on the role of existing institutions of higher education, the readiness of their core personnel to embrace change, and their capacity for effective agency.

- **Digital transition.** The world of education is taking part in the same rapid transition to digital media as the rest of society and cannot stand apart from it, regardless of its appetite for change in other areas. This transition does not in itself drive changes that are necessarily beneficial for education. It can lead to turmoil and increased costs, but as well it can hold out possibilities for cost savings and improvements in educational delivery. Either way, it is a force to be reckoned with.

- **Technology-enabled learning.** The transition to digital technology is setting the scene for a much deeper use of computing to drive interactive teaching and learning, supported by a rapidly growing body of research in learning science. There are still many uncertainties about how this knowledge and the new tools that support it will develop in practice. There is still much that is not yet settled. For example: How effective will big data be in driving education improvement? What are the privacy implications of collecting personal data? How responsive will faculty and administration be to using data to support instruction and students? What is the extent to which interactive content needs deep and expert curation? What is the role of place, the campus, the classroom? And so on.

It also became clear that, given the importance of digital technology in both creating momentum for change and opening up fundamentally new ways of learning, the role of industry-leading technology platform providers is a major factor shaping the future ecosystem of educational content and applications within which all other companies will operate. These platforms also open up new ways for education to be delivered by many other entrants to the educational arena—profit and nonprofit, public and private. Indeed, there is now a lively venture capital scene placing large investments in new entrants.

The two technology factors connect back to the first factor—the extent and pace of renewal in the institutions of higher education. Will they move ahead and capture the potential of technology for renewal, or will they be held back by longstanding structural challenges such that they are driven by the wave of change rather than riding it? Ultimately it is faculty, teachers, who are key actors in this process of change. They too must reach their own judgment about how best to harness the benefits of technology and embrace it in their practice to enhance their teaching and improve the effectiveness of the learning experience for their students.

PREDETERMINED ELEMENTS

These then are critical dynamics shaping the future for higher education as revealed by an initial Three Horizons mapping of the landscape. A closer look at the activities already in play in the Second Horizon transition space allows for a more granular view.

In classic futures practice it is common to map critical factors that have come up in the conversation against an impact-uncertainty grid. Those factors that are highly impactful and highly uncertain are set aside for further research as "critical uncertainties." Those that are highly impactful and with high predictability (low uncertainty) are likely to be predetermined elements, the importance of which was highlighted in the previous chapter.

In this case the process eventually identified 12 predetermined elements that are going to drive change in any scenario—and that any transformative Third Horizon vision will need to incorporate or contend with if it is to be realized. These are predetermined trends, already evident in the landscape. Those seeking to navigate the future will be wise to assume that these trends are not going away.

1. **Pressure for ROI increases.** With the cost of degrees increasing (around five times the rate of inflation since the early 1980s) and graduate salaries flat for much of the same period, the return on investment (ROI) in education is in question. U.S. student debt is now over $1 trillion. And the old model of guaranteed long-term employment is breaking down. So college-age students are seeing a lower ROI and a greater risk in studying at college. For successful graduates the rate of unemployment is low and the ROI still positive; the economic

risk is mostly for the 70 percent of students who fail to complete community college in three years and for the 40 percent who fail to complete a full four-year degree in six years. For these students, the debt is more burdensome, and they have a lower ability to secure the higher-paid jobs. At the same time, there is a growing need to provide resources for lifetime training and retraining—not just college education for 18- to 22-year-olds. Overall, there will be continuing pressure for lower costs, improved outcomes, and patterns of flexible, just-in-time education to meet the demands of the modern economy.

2. **Technology impact grows.** Already around 80 percent of college students own a laptop, and 70 percent own a smartphone. The point is not far off where every student will have a device and connectivity. The number of students doing at least one course online is steadily growing (it sits now at around 30 percent of students) and shows no sign of plateauing. Online outcomes are now fully comparable with classroom outcomes, and there are strong financial incentives to favor the former. Nearly all classroom content is already digital and is becoming richer, more interactive, and more adaptive.

3. **Focus on student outcomes is greater.** While there is considerable debate about what constitutes success for students and about the role of teachers, family, background, environment, technology, and so on in achieving it, it is clear that a focus on outcomes is now an embedded part of the culture of higher education. Many U.S. states are starting to base funding on student performance. That pressure is also coming from employers keen to fill significant skills gaps in the

U.S. economy. The trend toward a greater use of data analytics is well established in the consumer sector and is now being used in education to drive performance in key outcomes around student retention and student success. This is closely related to the following factor of data-driven approaches to learning and teaching, and will also drive changes in the role of administration to spot problems developing in student engagement and progress and provide appropriate support.

4. **Data-driven learning and teaching deliver results.** Studies to date are demonstrating how effective data-driven learning and teaching can be. Learning software is already proving its effectiveness, both in terms of the machine learning that allows software to improve its own targeted effectiveness (and improve its own content) in response to big data and also in terms of the capacity of applications to tailor output to the responses of individual students. Surveys are showing that adding a digital element to learning improves retention rates, course pass rates, and average exam scores. And students themselves are reporting that engagement with technology as part of their learning makes them more effective and efficient, increasing their interaction with fellow students, with their teachers, and with the content.

5. **Content and delivery channels will be disrupted while new print declines.** The increasing availability of digital options to complement or supplement print is causing disruption. Teaching and learning are changing as students and faculty adapt to new options for both. Google Apps for Education, for example, launched in 2008, is growing at an accelerating rate, adding over 5 million users a year. The disruption in provision of both con-

tent and delivery, familiar from music and other publishing, will continue to surge through the education sector. As this shift works its way through the system, it will enable and require a reassessment of the role of long-form reading alongside other instructional modalities such as augmented and virtual reality in support of teaching and learning. Innovation in these areas will further disrupt conventional content and delivery channels.

6. **Micro-credentialing is on the rise.** The Carnegie credit hour system has prevailed for over 100 years and is still foundational for many aspects of college life such as allocating resources, paying faculty, measuring student progress, etc. But now other ways of measuring and acknowledging progress are on the rise. The award of badges or other micro-credentials, authorized in a variety of ways, for the completion of short courses or the mastery of small packets of knowledge is in tune with a culture of instant ratings ("likes") and performance feedback (TripAdvisor) facilitated by connectivity and community. It is also a logical assessment strategy for competency-based learning (i.e., moving away from hours completed) and allows for flexibility for the learner to record progress over time and between numerous institutions and settings. Many business models are emerging. Start-ups promising ways to keep track of and validate credentials have raised big initial investments. Micro-credentialing is on the rise, and the conventional CV or résumé will give way to new forms of personal e-portfolios.

7. **Learning remains a social activity.** However effective personalized online learning has become, students still value the social dimensions of learning with others,

select their institution of learning based on its reputation for social activities, and in poll after poll confirm that they do not want exclusively online courses. Many of the skills most valued by employers are social skills rather than technical—skills like communication, teamwork, and leadership. There is also good evidence that the presence of an instructor improves outcomes through their social presence, independent of the quality of the content. Based on both research evidence and demand, we can expect learning to continue to be a social activity. However, as the next generation of digital natives grows up, much of their social activity will have migrated online, and there will have been continuing innovation in how to create online the social dimensions of learning that currently require shared physical presence. Just as with content, the online experience will open up fresh possibilities for the social dimensions of learning that will shift the relationship with the physical world and disrupt conventional modes of delivery.

8. **Privacy and compliance demands grow.** While it is true that the range of content that young people are willing to post online has been growing over the years, there are signs of a more reflexive and familiar generation beginning to become more cautious. Sharing information has always been fundamental to education, but most agree that personal information relating to students should not be widely shared and should not be mined for commercial gain. Data breaches in higher education became prevalent beginning in the mid-2000s, and over the following decade many institutions have established better processes and protocols

for collecting and using students' personal information. This has led to a sharp reduction in the number of data breaches in recent years. The Family Educational Rights and Privacy Act (FERPA) of 1974 imposes requirements on higher education institutions regarding how student personal information is handled. As the use of personalized student data to help improve learning outcomes grows, it will remain incumbent on higher education institutions to ensure that this information is protected.

9. **Education "wants to be free"—at least to the user.** Partly this is a statement of natural philosophy: education should be a right. It is reinforced in the "Google generation" for whom anything found on the Internet is expected to be free by default. Existing free-to-user education models draw on a number of sources, from government funds to private initiatives (think Google Apps for Education, iTunes U, edX), which either provide education as a public good or invest in education as a way to build a user base for other paid-for products. There is no shortage of models (philanthropic or other) to sustain "good enough" free-to-student education into the future. However, this is an area in transition. Many of the initiatives have very little momentum, and no stable model has become visible that will shape the whole sector. In addition, we can see in the willingness of people to pay for recognized accreditation that the dynamics around, and components of, what constitutes "education" in higher education are more complex than in K-12. Indeed the very poor completion rates (less than 5 percent) for the first generation of free massive open online courses, or MOOCS, point to the fact

that free provision of content by itself does not sustain *accredited* education.

10. **Pressure to remove frictions in the system is increasing.** Everywhere in our daily lives we are looking for smooth interoperability and the avoidance of unnecessary friction and hassle. It is no different in education. One solution is the uniformity of a single platform, which absorbs the complexity of multiple devices, different content providers, and so on. An alternative, pursued by the nonprofit organization IMS Global, a learning consortium now with over 400 members, is an open but coordinated ecosystem that ensures compatibility and interoperability without monopoly. Somewhere between the proprietorial and the consortium platform lies the Learning Tools Interoperability (LTI) standard, adherence to which allows for seamless connection of web-based, externally hosted applications and content to user-facing platforms.

11. **Ages and states model is secure for K-8, but changing beyond that.** The ages and stages model of education has dominated for over a century in K-12. There are signs of it beginning to weaken in the upper reaches of high school—for example, in a number of high school redesign initiatives. Schools are also starting to use more personalized/adaptive technologies and more project, team, and challenge-based learning approaches that help get away from the old model of subject-by-subject teaching of a single-age cohort in a classroom with a single teacher. Even so, there remains a strong belief that education is essentially social and that this is best achieved in an ages and stages model, particularly in the early years. Grit and resilience are also thought to be better rein-

forced in formal group rather than personalized learning settings. All of which suggests that at least in the early stages of the school career we can expect the ages and stages model to prevail for a good while yet. However, while 82 percent of U.S. students do complete and graduate high school, that average figure can be misleading as success rates vary widely across the country, and completion rates drop very sharply in the next stage—in part reflecting the lack of consistency and preparation at high school. Thus as restructuring pressures grow in order to improve performance in these stages, this will to some extent work its way back down through the system.

12. **New politics emerge.** The political scene is becoming more complicated with the rise of powerful special interest groups and social media. The venture capital community, for example, invested over $1 billion in education in 2014. The Gates Foundation has donated over $2 billion to various educational initiatives. Conservative and religious groups are becoming vocal about education and curriculum in certain parts of the United States. And all this is on top of traditional political battles and disagreements between Republicans and Democrats at the national level, between competing mayoral candidates at the city level, and between the Department of Education and new for-profit initiatives in terms of regulatory scrutiny. Along with this, there are battles about the role of school choice and vouchers in public education in K-12 and continuing debates around how best to lead, manage, and assess teachers. This is a confusing and evolving landscape with powerful forces at work—including the deep wish of parents to secure the "best" for their children.

Alongside these predetermined factors that can be predicted with a high degree of certainty, there are many other *critical uncertainties* that are likely to be influential in the future but that are less predictable and could go either way.

For MHE three stood out. Since it is a provider of course materials, one of the big questions is, Who is going to choose and pay for the content? Is it going to be the individual learner or the faculty/institution? It is clear that both modes are in play, but they are changing at different rates in different places.

The second question is about the emergence of technology standards in the education field. In this period of rapid development with so much being invested by institutions in IT, with many ideas and players and so much corporate and venture capital in the marketplace, the overall picture is difficult to discern. But it is possible to see the beginnings of a set of core standards emerging: Will the ecosystem eventually cohere around these, or will it continue to fragment?

Third, what will be the nature of the education marketplace? Will it be free, open, and competitive? Or will it become dominated by a few big providers? Note that by "marketplace" we mean a lot more than instructional materials, which are only about 2 percent of educational spending. The whole ecosystem of educational delivery—the other 98 percent of spending—is in play, and already we are beginning to see a small number of powerful players becoming prominent.

THREE SCENARIOS

The interplay of these three critical uncertainties alongside the predetermined elements suggests a number of possible scenarios for the future. MHE chose to focus on three of these, providing distinct, plausible, relevant, and challenging readings of how the landscape of higher education might evolve in the years ahead. Each takes a different view of which way the critical uncertainties might fall (Figure 2.2). Each roughly corresponds to the dominant voice of one of the Three Horizons: the manager renewing the system, the entrepreneur disrupting it, and the visionary shifting the paradigm.

The first scenario results when the institutions of higher education renew themselves, refreshing their role and fully adopting the changes enabled by technology to reduce costs, improve teaching, and extend their role in society to lifelong learning, holistic education, and job readiness. It is called "Renewal from Within."

If the institutions of higher education do not take the lead themselves, then two other plausible scenarios might result. If the institutions lag behind the pace of change, either

Renewal from Within	Education Remix	Big Tech Platforms

Institutions innovate	Entrepreneurs provide choice	Big tech firms dominate
Lower prices	Multiple price points	Lower costs
Academic reform	Micro-credentialing	Data-driven
Open platforms/ standards	Survival of fittest	Integrated platforms

FIGURE 2.2 **Three scenarios for the future of higher education— a headline view of three different trajectories for higher education depending on who takes the lead in creating the future.** (©2016, McGraw-Hill Education, Future of Higher Education)

they are likely to be "unbundled and rebundled" in the resulting frenzy of new entrants and new models, or they will effectively become beholden to whichever technology platform they choose to buy into. Hence, two further scenarios: "Education Remix" and "Big Tech Platforms."

Each scenario is set out below—including the underlying assumptions about critical uncertainties and examples of "pockets of the future in the present": real examples from present practice that suggest this scenario, this version of the future, is already under way.

Scenario 1: Renewal from Within

Critical Uncertainties

> *Content selection:* Institution or faculty led
>
> *Technology and education standards:* Convergent
>
> *Educational ecosystem:* Competitive

This scenario describes a world where educational institutions themselves drive the renewal in higher education to address cost pressures and student outcomes issues. We see more collaboration between traditional colleges and education technology entrepreneurs since the entrepreneurs are not trying to disrupt or disintermediate the colleges but to work with the existing infrastructure. Schools and colleges that best adopt innovations and turn them to their advantage will shape a future that embraces digital learning, competency-based credentialing and accreditation, and open platforms. What results is a thriving education ecosystem in which schools and colleges remain the principal providers and where there are more student transfers as it becomes easier for a student to take credits from one university to another.

The one-size-fits-all two-year or four-year degree erodes in its importance, and the open competitive marketplace means that education costs are reduced but there are fewer colleges as poor performers are weeded out.

We might see the following features emerge in this landscape:

- Colleges are squeezed as their funding changes and so colleges/schools/states start to collaborate in order to reduce costs and to build their relative power in the marketplace.

- Technology is widely adopted to reduce costs and improve student outcomes.

- Blended teaching models (using online and in-person teaching techniques) and flipped classrooms (where the class is used for active problem solving) become the norm—all harnessing adaptive learning solutions and an active use of data to support instruction.

- Interoperable (open) tech standards achieve critical mass and enable many different innovators to contribute to the ecosystem.

- Big tech players support the educational ecosystem and commit to join and build one platform standard (e.g., IMS Global).

- Students have more choice, at lower cost, leading to more enrollments, not just at ages 18–22 but through life.

- Colleges and accreditation bodies progressively adopt competency-based credentialing. Existing higher education brands prove to be a strong and recognized support for those credentials.

- The ROI for students from the brands and networks of the established institutions remains strong and positive—and value flows back toward them.

- Faculty remain important as they increasingly adapt to using data, flipped classrooms, and precision learning science and generally embrace technology and change.

Pockets of the Future

Arizona State University (ASU) has launched Global Freshman Academy in partnership with edX. Students can enroll in Global Freshman Academy from anywhere in the world. They can take ASU freshman courses for free and only pay if they have passed the course and want to receive university credit. They then pay only around $300 per credit unit, which they can use at ASU or at other institutions. This innovation is radically reducing both the cost to the student of getting a credit unit and the risk associated with failing or dropping out.

Georgia State University is a member of the University Innovation Alliance, a coalition of 11 public research universities "engaging in a public experiment to change the way universities work together and help more students achieve a quality college degree."[2] Starting in 2012, Georgia State has made a significant investment in predictive analytics to improve student outcomes and graduation rates. The university gathers information on 800 risk factors for each of its 50,000 students; it updates the information continuously and provides early feedback to a team of advisors who then meet with the relevant student to help keep things on track. The results have been impressive, including participation in

2 See www.theuia.org

the challenging STEM subjects (science, technology, engineering, and mathematics). Enrollment from low-income and nonwhite communities is up, and success for that student population in the STEM subjects is two to three times higher than five years ago. More than 90 percent of the cost of the project has been in staffing. There is no point having lots of information without people to interpret and respond to it. The university hired 42 new advisors at the start of the project at a cost of $2.5 million per year. That investment has been more than recouped in the estimated $10 million increase in income from enrollments and the fact that fewer students are dropping out. Students too have benefited, with a saving of an estimated $12 million since graduates are getting their degree on average half a semester sooner.

The IMS Global Learning Consortium is a nonprofit alliance of educational technology suppliers, institutions, districts, and states, all the main actors in the education ecosystem. It has grown rapidly to over 400 members. The consortium sets and certifies LTI standards so that applications developed for one specific instance can be used in a different instance or can be used in conjunction with different products. The aim is that the standards enable a simple, integrated, "plug-and-play" educational ecosystem.

Scenario 2: Education Remix

Critical Uncertainties

Content selection: Individual learner

Technology and education standards: Convergent

Educational ecosystem: Competitive with emerging oligopoly

This second scenario describes a consumer-driven world in which the traditional formality and constructs of learning are replaced by unbundled offerings focused on specific competencies. Entrepreneurs get to focus on discrete aspects of learning. You don't need to be a degree-bearing institution to certify a specific skill or area of competence. As a result, learners have much more choice at different price points. This pattern emerges from a renewed focus on lifelong learning, lines blurring between learning and work, and the simple fact that the current educational paradigm is increasingly expensive and decreasingly effective at achieving the desired results for students. Micro-credentialing and badging are commonplace and seen as legitimate by employers. Data influence decisions, and students take an active role in understanding and managing their own education, including owning and managing their own data. Accreditation as we know it has lost its chokehold in this world. The slow-paced governance model of higher education coupled with the role of accreditors and state-based funding means the sector has failed to adapt and is substantially replaced.

Some of the following features might be visible in this landscape:

- Students have the ability to pursue a self-selected educational path paved with badges and competency-based learning at a fraction of the cost of the traditional higher education model. Changing jobs and plotting a lifelong path through employment have also become easier with this highly flexible but recognized way of building up a portfolio of attested competencies.

- Micro-credentialing and badging are viable and widely accepted alternatives to the pursuit of a traditional degree.

- The learning process is everywhere, and from an early age, influenced by learning science and data derived from technology embedded in the learning process itself.

- Corporations regularly engage learning science companies to develop courses with curated content on their behalf to facilitate the identification of talent, accelerate the development of needed skill sets in the workplace, and augment their existing workforce competencies.

- This world is likely to be characterized in time by an oligopoly with converged standards dominated by a few highly visible micro-credentialing agencies, but alternatives will still exist and compete for legitimacy, including e-portfolio companies.

- Teachers will still be relevant, but they are more likely to participate in the "one-to-many" format in which discipline experts reach large numbers across multiple platforms and institutions. The number of tenured faculty will decline giving way to more facilitator roles, blended education, and making sure that learning remains social.

- Only those institutions with high external reputations, strong alumni networks, and sufficient endowment funds to withstand prolonged periods of principal drawdown will continue to provide the traditional higher education experience.

Pockets of the Future

General Assembly is a company offering training in 20 campus locations worldwide in six specialist areas matched to the demands of the technological economy. The courses are usually 12 weeks long and are tightly focused on how to code, how to design, and so on. The company enjoys close relationships with relevant employers. Some 90 percent of those enrolling in order to find jobs for the skills they develop are successful in doing so through General Assembly within 90 days of graduation. This is a company that's growing at a tremendous rate in terms of both student enrollment and investment income.

Udacity is now partnering with Google to offer a series of co-designed "nanodegrees." These are short courses, usually under a year and some as short as a month. Google has identified a shortage of Android developers. Through Udacity it is now offering a route for people to become certified in all aspects of Android development plus web development, virtual reality, and other specialist areas. The program has a laser-sharp focus on the skills market, and for its Nanodegree Plus program it offers a 100 percent refund in fees if the graduate does not land a job within six months.

Lynda provides short-form online video courses relevant to creative, business, and technology work. The courses can be an hour long broken into two- to three-minute chunks. There are very specific skills: for example for Microsoft Excel and how to use pivot tables. LinkedIn acquired the company in 2015 to form LinkedIn Learning. This means that Lynda courses are now integrated with the LinkedIn platform. Courses can be recommended to you based on your profile, positions that you might want to apply for can be linked not only to a list of skills requirements but also to the courses to acquire them, and if you do take a course, it is easy to add the resulting skills to your profile.

Scenario 3: Big Tech Platforms

Critical Uncertainties

Content selection: Institution

Technology and education standards: Fragmented

Educational ecosystem: Oligopoly

In this third scenario, we imagine a world in which the big tech companies drive the future. This is a world in which both schools and colleges (K-20 education institutions) are increasingly under pressure to manage their costs, to provide accessibility at home and on campus, and to demonstrate successful learning outcomes—a tangible return on investment—against ever more detailed metrics. There is also pressure from students educated in a single-provider, big tech environment in K-12 to replicate that environment in higher education. In this future scenario, big tech companies like Google, Microsoft and Amazon would therefore offer "school systems" that integrate seamless school technologies with cloud hosting to manage both learning and school administration—the school information system (SIS) and the learning management system (LMS). For the institution, this is an attractive solution to the confusing mess of technology offers, standards, prices, metrics, and the need to transfer grades and other data seamlessly from one year to the next. Colleges and schools will partner with their chosen big tech supplier to adopt a system that becomes the institution's single platform. Each school system collects data on students and faculty that are used to increase efficiencies, improve outcomes, and demonstrate success. But the standards that work on one platform do not transfer across to another. Just as in the world of cell phones, you are either a Verizon customer or an AT&T customer, and they don't interoperate, so in this world we can expect a highly oligopolistic market dominated by a few big tech companies.

Note that this is just a scenario, not a description of the existing level of integration or of any known or stated plans of technology companies. But it is a plausible future given where we are today and might include the following features:

- Google, Amazon and Microsoft offer end-to-end solutions as "loss leaders" to reduce education institutions' costs, capturing students before they enter the workplace and encouraging them to become loyal future users.

- Data privacy issues are addressed so that big data solutions (particularly around longitudinal data) become viable and socially acceptable.

- The breadth of IT needs for institutions of higher education—hosting, support, devices, platforms, data analysis—precludes all but the largest tech companies from competing for the business.

- Interventions with students are personalized and prompted by the data and are delivered either through the technology or through teacher action guided by insight from the data.

- K-12 and higher education completion rates significantly improve as big tech platform end-to-end solutions provide effective early warning systems throughout a student's academic career.

- More affordable educational technology, coupled with stable and reliable operating platforms, leads to a dramatic increase in technology adoption and usage.

Pockets of the Future

AWS Educate makes Amazon's cloud-based web services capability available to academia, teachers, and students. Amazon Inspire is a library of digital learning resources for K-12 that will soon include "share" and "rate" functions for crowd-sourced content. Amazon Education Publishing allows educators to create, publish, and share print books, e-books, audiobooks, and video content. Kindle Whispercast is a free platform for schools to deliver digital content to students across multiple devices.

Google Apps for Education offers a suite of free web-based collaborative study solutions across devices. In just five years, usage has grown to the point where in 2017 more than half of the primary and secondary school students in the United States were using Google education apps. The Google-powered Chromebook now accounts for more than half of the devices shipped to U.S. schools. Google Classroom is a free content management system, a "mission control for class." Teachers are offered training, certification, membership in Google Educator Groups worldwide, and invitations to more exclusive leadership symposiums.

Microsoft provides teachers and students at qualifying schools in the United States free access to Office 365 Education including Teams and OneNote. The company has an extensive range of free apps for supporting education and promoting creativity as parts of an integrated suite that includes Skype and the popular Minecraft learning game. Teachers are offered free training and can take courses to earn points and badges toward certification as an MIE (Microsoft Innovative Educator).

....

Obviously these three scenarios are not mutually exclusive, and the sector is big enough for them to coexist to a significant extent. They all might play out with varying degrees of emphasis across the sector. But they do provide three useful navigational aids for institutions of higher education.

In conversations introducing these scenarios since 2014, MHE has found that many investors, education institutions, and technology providers have been assuming just one of these as the future. Bringing all three into view, particularly the encouragement for the institutions themselves in "Renewal from Within," makes it possible to have a much richer conversation about the way ahead.

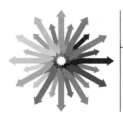

CHAPTER THREE

FROM INSIGHT TO ACTION

We have introduced in the previous chapter three scenarios developed with and by MHE as a way of exploring the nature of the immediate landscape ahead in higher education, the predetermined elements, the uncertainties, and three richly researched, evidence-based, plausible stories for how the future might unfold over the next 5 to 10 years.

The next step, moving into the space of truly "reflexive futures," is to put ourselves in the picture. We are not only responding to this emerging environment, but through our own actions we are shaping it. Remember, the essence of transformative innovation is to help shift the system toward new patterns of viability fit for the future and in tune with our own aspirations.

So, having taken stock of the emerging landscape with its sources of concern, its trends, its uncertainties, its pockets of the future in the present, and so on, the next challenge is to devise innovation pathways to catch the wave of change and navigate the turbulent transition toward a Third Horizon of our own choosing. This chapter describes three steps toward achieving that objective:

1. Put our values in the picture.

2. Identify navigational dilemmas.

3. Get into action.

PUTTING OUR VALUES IN THE PICTURE

From the perspective of an existing institution of higher education, some of the predetermined elements discussed in the previous chapter, and indeed some aspects of the scenarios derived from them and other critical factors, may be a little alarming. Even so, they cannot be ignored. The task of transformation is to realize a specific vision of the future in the context of powerful and predictable forces and the vision and actions of other players.

The conversation about vision and aspiration will be distinctive in each institution. But we can be sure that, in a changing world, it will inevitably reveal tensions between the way things are now and what that institution aspires to in the future. There might be discussions about the need to follow the money and the market, or to "restore the soul" of the college's founding vocation, or to equip young people with the resilience they need for a confusing world rather than the microcredentials they need for the next job. Such conversations will be familiar to anybody active in higher education today. Underpinning them are fundamental tensions about values.

One simple reading of the Three Horizons transition is that a set of structures has grown over time to create a stable and reliable pattern in the First Horizon. But those structures have inevitably made some values—like reliability and efficiency—more realizable than others—like personalization and flexibility.

The path of transformative innovation involves recovering those neglected values and growing new patterns and structures to realize them reliably in the future. At the same time the system as a whole needs to find a place in the future for the positive values of the First Horizon—the baby that must not be thrown out with the bathwater. It is not that we can do without values of reliability and efficiency; it is just that we no longer feel able to realize our full aspirations in a system dominated by those values seemingly to the exclusion of others.

The overall trajectory of the transition is represented in Figure 3.1. In effect, the First Horizon pattern moves over time from structures to values, while the new Third Horizon pattern grows from values to structures.

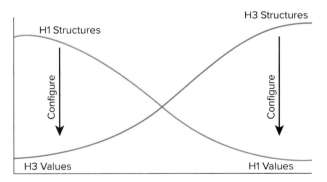

FIGURE 3.1 **The relationship between values and structures.** At present the structures of the First Horizon configure (and usually constrain) the values of the Third. In the future those Third Horizon values inform the dominant structures that now configure (and constrain) the values of the First.

In diverse conversations with institutions of higher education about the scenarios in the previous chapter, it has been possible to start to get a sense of this direction of travel from the perspective of the system itself. Naturally the desirable future will look different for different institutions and will depend also to an extent on the passions, roles, and experience of those involved in the conversation. But for the purposes of illustrating how to move from a conversation that locates an institution in its landscape of change to taking effective transformative action, we might take the characteristics of a desirable Third Horizon that follow as typical.

These are real observations from real conversations involving a range of institutions, clustered together here for the sake of identifying core characteristics. These are the characteristics that the institutions involved would like to see emerge from the shifting landscape described in the previous chapter. Some are more easily realizable in one scenario than in others. But the point of the exercise is to engage with the substance of the emerging future and to determine an institutional vision in response—not simply to adapt effectively to one world or another.

Here then are some of the features of a desirable Third Horizon pattern identified in conversation with existing institutions of higher education. They offer an indication of a desired direction of travel.

Person-Centered Holistic Education

Vocational education and technical education are valued in a holistic perspective.

T-shaped people: people have a foundational education plus an infinite variety of badges.

Education is genuinely episodic.

The well-educated plumber—the student learns a trade and skills plus other attributes.

Ages and stages give way to anytime learning and peer-to-peer support.

Education is genuinely lifelong.

Technology shifts the curve toward mastery-based education for all.

A holistic view of education is the norm.

Students invest in their own education—throughout life.

The student is in charge—learning is personalized.

Learning is self-assembled, and so are learning communities.

Education provides wisdom, not just a skill.

Education and Employment Aligned and Boundaries Blurred

The context is global: the market for skills and employment is open.

Relevance to the world of work flows through tech platforms.

Students learn through experience, hands on, with others.

Students learn credited skills that can be presented to employers.

Employers can now reliably hire people who will succeed.

Education and the world of work are aligned.

The data ecosystem brings students' and employers' needs closer together.

The blend of work experience and formalized education keeps colleges "in touch" and relevant.

Simple, Stable, Reliable, Inexpensive Platforms

Big tech comes in behind accredited institutions and empowers them.

Costs are down; complexity is down.

Tech makes the trains run on time—a utility, as natural as e-mail.

There is no need for a CTO/IT department: technology confusion is outsourced.

The lights will stay on—cost pressures are resolved.

Faculty are free to support students (no need to worry about interoperability).

Faculty are released from confusion by stable, single platforms.

Amazon world, Google world, Microsoft world: big tech providers offer a simple landscape.

Integration and curation of modules comes for free (via platform).

Quality Education with No Price Barrier

Cost is lower, quality is higher, and there is greater student satisfaction.

The right students get the right education at the right cost.

There is a great value proposition for students.

Costs are low enough to allow "education for its own sake."

A unique educational experience is delivered to each individual.

Retention is enhanced—data flows, early warnings, and personal support contribute.

Formative data constantly feed back to students and faculty to improve performance.

Social, Playful Learning

The gaming paradigm is set free: learning is fun and immersive.

VR and AR enhance the student experience: "place" is naturally expanded.

The social process of learning is renewed.

The campus still exists—open and social.

Technology enhances the educational experience.

Learning is online and face-to-face: the social aspects and informal learning are artfully blended.

Open Culture of Exploration and Mastery

Collaboration—faculty and students—is natural and enhanced.

There are faculty-supported communities of practice.

Access to mastery becomes more available—"rock star" faculty.

Faculty come out of the ivory tower.

People understand education is of value both for the economy and for global citizenship.

Richness is restored.

Education serves as ethical leader.

Students are genuinely engaged with content.

Exploration is valued—as well as resilience and persistence.

These then are some of the characteristics identified for a desired Third Horizon pattern, to be delivered by a stable and reliable set of structures in the future. What then are the values that underpin this pattern? If these are the desired characteristics of a new system, what can we say that system values? This may take a little work, but it should be possible to identify a pattern of values working through the list cluster by cluster.

For example:

- Person-centered holistic education—underpinned by a commitment to *a focus on the person* and to *a broad holistic curriculum*

- Education and employment aligned and boundaries blurred—underpinned by a commitment to *relevant and flexible education for the real world*

- Simple, stable, reliable, inexpensive platforms—underpinned by a commitment to *a focus on education, not administration*

- Quality education with no price barrier—underpinned by a commitment to *high-quality education for all*

- Social, playful learning—underpinned by a commitment to *creativity and natural curiosity*

- Open culture of exploration and mastery—underpinned by a commitment to *discovery and exploration* and to *depth of learning*

These are not "new" values as such. We are committed to them in the existing First Horizon, but they are not necessarily supported by the structures that have grown up over time to support that system. Indeed, they can often be experienced as existing in tension with other values that are closer to the core of First Horizon concerns. That is why it is so useful to identify the equivalent First Horizon value that often holds us back whenever we seek to move to realize more of the Third.

The most effective way to identify these value tensions might be to bring the whole conversation back into the present and to role-play a conversation between a Third Horizon "visionary" advocating for the values above and a well-disposed First Horizon "manager" ready to adopt a positive perspective in that conversation (see Figure 1.6). If you were to argue for more room for discovery, exploration, and depth of learning in the curriculum, what might a hard-pressed First Horizon manager trying to keep the institution afloat have to say? If the manager is well disposed, what he or she says will be positive rather than just obstructive—and will reveal the positive value in the existing First Horizon system to range against the value in the Third. If we repeat that exercise for all the values underpinning our desired Third Horizon pattern, we might end up with a list of value tensions something like the ones shown in Table 3.1.

TABLE 3.1 **Value Tensions Between First and Third Horizon Patterns**

First Horizon Value	Third Horizon Value
A focus on the ongoing viability of the system	*A focus on the person*
A specialized curriculum to meet expressed demand	*A broad holistic curriculum*
Education as relevant and flexible as possible within budget constraints	*Relevant and flexible education for the real world*
A focus on administration; otherwise there will be no education	*A focus on education, not administration*
Some level of education for all or high-quality education for some (within budget constraints)	*High quality education for all*
Core, fundamental skills	*Creativity and natural curiosity*
Learning what is already known	*Discovery and exploration*
Broad, general education	*Depth of learning*

Some of the "tensions" identified in the table may be easily resolved. For example, it seems clear that we will always need a system that works for both administration and education. Relevant, flexible education for the real world may likewise be a shared value across all the Horizons. The reason why these values are in tension and not in conflict is that *both* sets are desirable.

Some of the value tensions will be more difficult to resolve than others. If we can find those deep tensions in the Three Horizons conversation, it will prove particularly valuable—since it is these tensions, expressed as dilemmas, that in practice provide both a sense of direction for transformative innovation and the motive power to propel an institution toward it.

Figure 3.2 shows the results of this exercise in another context—addressing the overcrowding of hospitals during the winter months in one region of Scotland. The senior managers involved developed their own Three Horizons map of the landscape, clustered the characteristics of their desired Third Horizon, identified the values underpinning that new pattern, and then determined where those values were in tension with other worthwhile values in the existing system.

Having identified these value tensions, it is then possible to come up with promising innovation pathways to lead the transition from one pattern to the other: growing the workforce to participate in the new system, for example, or evolving technology to give it "a human face."

We can follow the same process with the analysis from higher education in Table 3.1. Figure 3.3 shows the results.

The best way to complete the exercise to identify the H2 innovation pathways is to use another powerful framework to explore these value tensions in practice. We need to address them as navigational dilemmas.

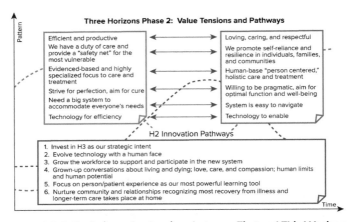

FIGURE 3.2 **Exploring value tensions between First and Third Horizon patterns.** This exercise, conducted to explore a shift in the provision of health and social care in a region of Scotland, reveals a number of promising innovation pathways to move towards a third horizon aspiration. (See *Shine: Changing The Culture of Care—A Case Study of Systems Change*, International Futures Forum, 2018)

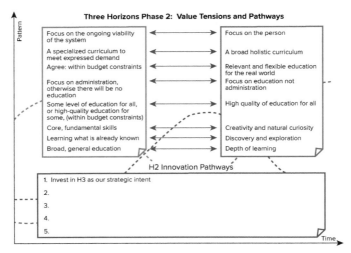

FIGURE 3.3 **Value tensions in the landscape of higher education.** What are the innovation pathways that they suggest?

IDENTIFYING NAVIGATIONAL DILEMMAS

Dilemma thinking was pioneered by the management theorist Charles Hampden-Turner[1] and has been substantially developed in practice by our IFF colleague Anthony Hodgson. The characteristic of a dilemma is precisely that it tugs us between two positive values where a simple choice is inadequate. We want both structure and freedom, for example, or a job that gives us both money and meaning. If we place these values not at different ends of a spectrum but at right angles, we create a "dilemma space" with a sweet spot in which we can combine the best of *both* values—where we can have our cake and eat it.

This is precisely the nature of the transition zone between the First and Third Horizons. We take a stand for a pattern of values that are undervalued in the First Horizon, and we wish to transform the system to create reliable patterns in which those values can flourish. Yet at the same time there are values in the First Horizon system that will still be needed in the future. The transition must be toward a "both/and" pattern, not an "either/or."

That is one reason why so many conversations about the future in higher education seem to go around in circles. When it comes to dilemmas, both sides of the argument are right. We cannot neglect short-term financial viability. But at the same time neither can we neglect longer-term exploration around the changing needs of the student population. It is no good keeping the lights on today if we are going to be left in darkness as waves of change sweep over us in the next

---

1 See for example his books *Charting the Corporate Mind: From Dilemma to Strategy*, Oxford Blackwell (1990) and (with his long-term colleague and collaborator Fons Trompenaars) *Building Cross-Cultural Competence: How to Create Wealth from Conflicting Values*, Wiley (2000).

decade. Effective strategy, policy, and action need to confront these dilemmas in the transition zone rather than evade or succumb to them.

Most dilemmas take a similar form. There is generally a hard "rock value" with the quality of the immovable object on one horn and a softer "whirlpool value" with the quality of an irresistible force on the other. If we cling exclusively to either, then the other will find us out eventually. Thus a business might fail as easily by sticking rigidly to its core product as it might by putting all its resources into speculative innovation: this is a dilemma, not a choice, and needs to be managed as such.

Moving toward the resolution space, the best of both worlds, where $1 + 1 = 3$, is not a simple linear process. It is like tacking a sailboat against the wind. We may need to move toward the rock value for a while, before turning to introduce more of the whirlpool value.

This way of thinking is particularly useful in relation to the Three Horizons framework. As we have seen, there are likely to be tensions between the H1 business-as-usual system and the aspirational Third Horizon. The First Horizon works, the Third Horizon liberates—both good things. Even if they do not show up immediately in the conversation about an institution's strategy, there will almost certainly be value tensions in the wider world the institution has to navigate. A group seeking to shift the model of higher education toward the softer skills of compassion and inclusion, for example, will sooner or later have to reckon with others in the world applying their resources and energy to competing H3 visions of aggressive, winner takes-all-competition. We cannot ignore other voices and other perspectives.

Likewise, even if we are aligned around an aspirational vision of the Third Horizon, tensions are likely to arise about the best means to gain that end. Should we rely on the market or on state regulation, for example, and should our actions privilege local choice or global efficacy? Dilemmas abound, even when we are aligned on the purpose.

The smart H2+ policy course will be toward the point of dilemma resolution: consciously steering a path between two poles and using the tension between them as a source of propulsion, a motive force to determine the direction of travel toward the creative resolution of the Third Horizon. That is why we call these "navigational dilemmas."

There are five possible outcomes in managing a dilemma (Figure 3.4). If we stick to the rock value, we will become a dinosaur and die out. If we stick to the whirlpool value, we become a unicorn—a mythical beast that could never survive in the real world. If we compromise, we end up as an ostrich, head in the sand. If we get stuck in the zone of conflict, we will be like Dr. Doolittle's pushmi-pullyu. But if we get to the resolution space, we will soar like an eagle.

To work through the critical dilemmas identified in a Three Horizons conversation, it is helpful to divide the dilemma space into five zones, corresponding to the zones shown in Figure 3.4. For the tension in question, we can then perform the following step-by-step analysis, working through the zones in order:

- **Zone 1.** State what is essential from this perspective. What would we do if we favored this perspective?

- **Zone 2.** State what is essential from this perspective. What would we do if we favored this perspective?

- **Zone 3.** What are the typical activities that arise from a compromise between the two values? How is the tension between them typically managed in practice?

- **Zone 4.** Where are the values in conflict? What are the (unresolved) arguments that currently take place between them?

- **Zone 5.** Seek creative resolution. What can the Zone 1 value offer the Zone 2 value without loss of integrity, and vice versa?

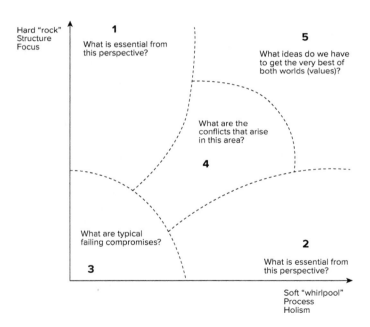

Hard "rock" Structure Focus

1
What is essential from this perspective?

5
What ideas do we have to get the very best of both worlds (values)?

What are the conflicts that arise in this area?

4

What are typical failing compromises?

3

2
What is essential from this perspective?

Soft "whirlpool" Process Holism

FIGURE 3.4 **The structure of a dilemma.** Dilemmas typically lie between a hard rock value and a softer whirlpool value. In resolving a dilemma there are four ways to fail (Zones 1 to 4) and only one way to succeed (Zone 5). (© International Futures Forum, 2009.)

What this exercise quickly brings out is the following:

- It is very easy to identify compromise solutions that suppress the tension without addressing it (Zone 3). It is much more difficult to get to the resolution space (Zone 5).

- A willingness to wrestle with and ride the horns of the dilemma in Zone 4 prevents the slip into easy compromise or the tendency to migrate to either pole of the discussion.

- It is interesting to find that wrestling with the dilemma and seeking creative ways of combining the best of both worlds often identifies existing practice that can now be seen in a new light—exemplifying the Third Horizon in the present. The future is already here, just unevenly distributed—but we first have to know what we are looking for.

Creative Integrity: Holding the Dilemma, Standing for the Future

Using navigational dilemmas to identify a sense of direction, the pathways to a Third Horizon, implies that there must also be a vehicle to make the journey. That is not likely in the first instance to be the entire staff of an institution. More common would be a core strategic group, a pioneering initiative, a small group of managers and practitioners empowered to lead the way for others to follow. We call this group a "creative integrity."

The word "integrity" arises quite naturally in the context of existing First Horizon systems. It is common and natural to identify such systems as reliable and stable. That is a defining quality. The First Horizon pattern, as we have said, is the domain of the manager. It is a pattern that people can be held responsible for and that we can therefore trust. When we go to the doctor, for example, we trust that he will prescribe the right drugs. Or when we take the car to the mechanic, we trust that she will not forget to fix the brakes. In this sense, integrity is about taking responsibility for maintaining a pattern that is already there. We call this a "patterned integrity."

If we are to champion the values of an aspirational Third Horizon, we need to stand aside from business as usual to embody and begin to realize a new pattern. This pattern will also have to maintain its integrity—this time more like a seed than an established system. We call this a "creative integrity"—a manifestation in the present of the Third Horizon potential. It is creative because it steps outside the existing patterns to stand for something different.

The creative integrity will both embody the desired future in the present (to show that it is possible) and also "hold" the dilemmas that will inevitably be encountered along the way. A dilemma is never fully resolved. There is no "solution." Rather, it implies two positive qualities that must always be held in tension, where the task is to reconcile them moment by moment without losing sight of the goal. It is the task of the creative integrity to hold the Second Horizon dilemmas and to resolve them in the moment, sometimes tacking toward the rock value, sometimes toward the whirlpool, on the emerging pathway to the Third Horizon.

While the dilemma is never resolved, we do find ourselves settling on structures that work for a time and that are an advance on other forms that have lost their capacity to work dynamically with both poles. That is what we are looking to establish with creative integrity: structures that can stabilize and grow and that are more appropriate to emerging times, even though we know that in another generation they will have to change again.

GETTING INTO ACTION

Once a group has its Three Horizons mapping in place, once it has scoped the territory and identified the navigational dilemmas to keep it on track, it will require individuals to absorb the implications and to develop the courage to make a first step into the unknown toward the Third Horizon. Equally the group needs to do so with discipline and with a plan that is rooted in the challenges of the real world, not the fantasy world of blue-sky magical thinking.

A range of conversational tools and frameworks is available to help.[2] There is no getting away from the fact that taking a step along the transformative innovation pathway is inherently risky. The dominant systems of the First Horizon are not designed to support such actions. At some level those actions will be seen as culturally transgressive. Hence the need to find ways to listen for and engage the voices of resistance and avoidance, the statements of possibility and experiment, and the pragmatic targets and investments and disciplines necessary to bring our aspirations to fruition.

All three of these perspectives, like the Three Horizons, will be present in the conversation about taking an initiative to change the system: it is important to listen to and work with them all. That is particularly true for the voice of resistance—the naysayers and the cynics. It is important to

---

2 IFF uses a set of powerful change tools developed by our colleague Jim Ewing that dovetail very nicely with the Three Horizons framework. See www.executivearts.co.uk.

include their energy in the conversation: it is extraordinary how potent a resource for change such people can become when they are really heard.

Both at the start of the process and at points along the way, we will find that there is a step to be taken, a move to be made, a decision about whether to steer toward this or that pole of the dilemma in this moment, and a degree of uncertainty about which way to go.

It helps to rehearse the potential moves ahead of time and then to use the learning from such conversations to redesign those moves to maximize the chances of success and mitigate the risk of failure. Most risk management conversations are so determined to mitigate or prevent risk that they render the next move impossible. By eliminating the most evident downside risks, they end up equally frustrating the upside potential. The fact of the matter is that transformative innovation is inherently risky: if you have eliminated the risk in the next step, then you are not doing it right.

The conversation therefore needs to consider equally both the best that might happen as a result of a move and the worst. And then it needs to consider what might be possible, in both situations. This can be particularly effective in dealing with our worst fears since, as our colleague Jim Ewing says, we are much better at solving problems with hindsight (after we have imagined them happening) than we are with foresight (planning to prevent them from happening).

One such conversation in a school, following a Three Horizons process, was about trying out a new approach to parents' evenings. This might seem a very small step, but it was a first move on the pathway of change and exposed the tensions the school was experiencing between the Horizon voices. A worst fear was that nobody would come, while the highest hope was that they couldn't find a room big enough to hold the throng. Clearly attendance and engagement were measures of success for the initiative. Both of these extremes were unlikely. So what would count as an acceptable minimum on a first outing for the new model? After some discussion, it was agreed that if six people came, that would at least be a start. Anything less would show that the idea was just not going to fly.

Without that conversation, the teachers might have been thoroughly dispirited when only eight people showed up on the night. But this was above their threshold, and so they chose to carry on. They certainly had to think hard about how to do better, but they were redesigning the initiative rather than abandoning it.

The essential requirement is to turn what is inevitably going to feel like a risky move into "managed risk" and therefore encourage people to make a move that previously might have looked far too scary. This approach will also work with whatever energy is in the group, including the energy of opposition. When the first step in the conversation is to ask "What is the worst that could happen?" and the process then treats the answers seriously, everyone becomes a participant.

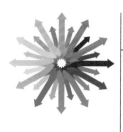

CHAPTER FOUR

SUPPORTING TRANSFORMATIVE INNOVATION

THREE HORIZONS INNOVATION STRATEGY

This book is about action. The previous chapter focused on how to move from the insights gained from a strategic conversation about the future into effective, transformative practice.

But we cannot neglect strategy and policy. There is always a larger landscape in play, one in which educational institutions themselves are not the principal actors. We have written elsewhere about how policy and finance can work better to support, rather than frustrate, transformative change.[1] The tools, processes, and approaches outlined so far can be very

---

1 "Enabling," Chapter 6 in *Transformative Innovation*, Graham Leicester, Triarchy Press (2016).

effectively deployed by governments, politicians, and policy professionals to bring their own practice into line with the demands of the turbulent times of the twenty-first century.

Closer to home the same applies to the senior managers and policy and strategy makers in our institutions of higher education and indeed across the sector. This final chapter offers some thoughts on the conditions they—and others—might put in place to support the realization of transformative change.

As a baseline, our work suggests that an effective policy framework within an institution and/or across the sector needs at least to facilitate the following five features.

1. A Compelling Vision of the Third Horizon

Without this vision, all innovation will be sucked back toward making the existing system work better (usually more efficiently). That has been the fate of many educational reform movements to date—churning the surface while leaving deep structures unchanged.

Envisioning a Third Horizon, fundamentally different from the first, opens up a space in which to design a longer-term transition from one dominant pattern of activity to another. It also sharpens our attention in the present so that we notice pockets of the future where this new, transformed culture is already in evidence in some places and at some scale (even when this is not in the field of education).

It is not unusual to find this vision already in place in policy statements. The world is littered with institutional visions for a better world, usually a decade or more away. What they tend to lack is any explicit acknowledgment that achieving such goals will require a radical transformation in existing patterns and culture. They can easily be interpreted—

and usually are—as a call for an adjustment and rebalance in existing provision rather than a wholesale shift to a new viable pattern. Without an explicit Third Horizon goal, all systems and resources will inevitably be skewed toward maintaining and improving the status quo.

It is the responsibility of those working at strategic or policy-making levels within the system to be aware of this dynamic. They need to be planning always both to keep the plane in the air and to redesign it. They will need to be adept at playing in both the First Horizon and the Third Horizon at the same time and conscious of the subtle, systems-level appreciation needed to create space for a new pattern to grow in the presence of the old and to enable a long-term transition from one to the other.

2. Encouragement for Pioneers

The Three Horizons framework describes and invites a journey from small beginnings toward a new, stable pattern that can reliably configure at least a part of the landscape of higher education for some time to come. Those ready to set out on such a journey and embody in the present a new way of doing things, however countercultural they may appear at the time, are our pioneers.

The problem for those in strategy and policy-making positions is what stance to adopt toward these apparent mavericks and misfits. We know that among their projects are the seeds of future viability. We understand the need for all three roles—"pioneers," "settlers," and "town planners"—as agents of effective systems change. And we know the quote often attributed to Gandhi about how agents of cultural change are often underestimated when they appear: "First they ignore you, then they laugh at you, then they fight you, then you win."

The difficulty is in knowing which of those pioneers always appearing on the fringes of any system are deserving of support—and then how to give it. If a clear vision of a Third Horizon is articulated at the policy and strategy level, then this is relatively straightforward.

First, the nature of the support need only take the form of permission to proceed, either explicit or implicit. Status quo, business-as-usual systems, institutions, and assumptions will naturally hold back, rein in, capture, co-opt, or fatally frustrate pioneering innovation that might otherwise have pointed to a different future. So the first requirement of policy and strategy is to acknowledge explicitly the need for more radical, pioneering innovation that will inevitably appear countercultural. That gives permission to the pioneers. At the outset, the role of First Horizon authority is simply not to say no—and ideally to provide the protected spaces and an environment within the institution where a new pattern is allowed to develop on its own terms and to grow.

Second, managerial policy makers will worry that encouraging the visionaries will fragment and diversify what are generally intended to be universal patterns and offerings. Hence "if we cannot do it for everyone, we should not do it for anyone." To overcome this mindset, the institution will need to become much more sophisticated about how it learns from experiment, how it extracts principles from one place to apply in another, and so on. Just as medicine is beginning to learn how to move beyond a monotheistic belief in randomized control trials and effectiveness based on averages drawn from big numbers, so too should policy become more adept at dealing with the unique, the personal, the specific, the set of $n = 1$.

Dilemma thinking (see the earlier section, "Identifying Navigational Dilemmas") is a particularly powerful tool for making this shift. As issues arise that look like choices between mutually exclusive goods—such as universality and diversity—management has two roles. The first is to make clear at what level in the institution the dilemma is held and therefore constantly addressed and resolved. The second is to practice dilemma thinking itself and to encourage it in others, in order to get the best of both worlds—generative resolution rather than simplistic choices or flawed compromise. The dilemma space is a space of innovation and creative resolution that will naturally generate scores of powerful ideas for unlocking diversity of provision within overall standards of universality. These are precisely the conditions that management needs to provide to stimulate innovation—conditions that unlock abundance, complexity, and life.

Third, those in strategic and policy-making positions might give active encouragement to pioneering initiatives that are consistent with their own stated Third Horizon aspirations. They should look particularly for such initiatives *within* their existing structures. They will always be there but are not nearly as visible as start-ups outside the system.

The nature of the encouragement in the early pioneering stage need be no more than appreciative attention: "We have seen what you are doing. It looks interesting. Carry on." But in order for a transformative initiative to complete the transition to form a new, stable, reliable pattern, a patterned integrity, there will come a time when, having started out by not saying no, systems of First Horizon authority actively have to say yes—and transfer resources to match.

3. A Realistic View of the Policy Landscape

With a Three Horizons view of the landscape, the power of sunk cost infrastructure in the patterns that sustain the First Horizon to constrain innovation becomes clear. As one senior participant offering H1 support for an innovation put it in a workshop we ran recently about healthcare: "Be aware that we have a black belt in taking promising organic initiatives and strangling the life out of them." This was Clayton Christensen's point about disruptive innovation. It is killed or ignored by managers, not because they are doing a bad job, but precisely because they are performing their First Horizon managerial role to perfection.

The equivalent in policy terms is to be found in Albert Hirschman's book *The Rhetoric of Reaction: Perversity, Futility, Jeopardy*. His research reveals three dominant patterns of the H1 argument against progressive innovation: *perversity* (it will have perverse effects beyond those intended), *futility* (it will have no effect), and *jeopardy* (it might work, but it puts previous success at risk). Both authors tap into a central truth of sound management: if there is tension between the new and the old, the radically different and the known, it must privilege the latter.

For the innovator, the challenge is not simply to innovate but to do so in such a way that longer-term evolution of the system will result—i.e., introducing the new in ways that allow it to flourish *in the presence of the old*. Policy and strategy must likewise acknowledge the real tensions and dilemmas of change, where both the existing system and the imagined future have merit and value. It must be ready to free up some of the intellectual, physical, and eventually financial resources currently locked into the maintenance and improvement of the existing system. It needs to give some support to H2 innovation with H3 aspirations, seeding creative resolution of the dilemmas even while the bulk of funding and management attention goes toward maintaining the present system.

4. Strategic Exemplification

Policy for innovation often follows a simple model of providing dedicated funds to support pilot projects, coupled with an investment in sharing best practice. The weakness in such a model can be a lack of strategic direction such that the landscape is littered with shiny, eye-catching initiatives but no overall systemic progress. With a Third Horizon vision and a realistic view of the policy landscape, it is possible to be much more intentional about the kind of innovations that are supported, identified, and shared. We need examples of Third Horizon practice in the present to inspire us. And we need examples of Second Horizon innovation that has the potential to ease the transition from the First Horizon toward the Third. We call this "strategic exemplification"—the highlighting of examples that are not just novel, different, or interesting but have true *strategic significance in the context of a stated Third Horizon vision.*

Equally we must recognize the inherent limitations of sharing best practice—typically associated with incremental improvement. As one workshop participant put it: "In a rapidly changing world, best practice is something that used to work, somewhere else." Transformative innovation is about inspiring, not replicating—which suggests much greater use of experiential learning journeys to visit pockets of the future in the present as a way of encouraging growth and development. These journeys need not be far from home.

5. Evaluation Based on Third Horizon Intentions

Evaluation is always going to be a problem for any innovation with transformative intent. It needs to usher in a new culture while accounting for its performance in terms of existing (H1) priorities and assumptions.

Transformative innovation cannot be evaluated simply according to the standards and processes of the First Horizon. But it must be evaluated—not only to encourage the innovators, but to retain credibility within H1 power structures. As Jim Collins says in his *Good to Great and the Social Sectors,* those who say that their version of success cannot be measured are guilty of intellectual laziness. Thinking about navigational dilemmas (see the earlier section, "Identifying Navigational Dilemmas") and the minimum acceptable outcome for a risky endeavor (see the earlier section, "Getting into Action"), we can see that both point to the importance in any event of our own intrinsic measures of success or failure in order to keep us on track.

An essential element of the practical transition toward an H3 vision should be a disciplined approach to self-evaluation that recognizes the value of experience and narrative alongside more conventional data. Transformative innovation should certainly measure indicators that matter to existing systems. But at the same time, those responsible for strategy and policy within those existing systems need somehow to acknowledge that the true value of such innovation (a) will not be realized immediately, (b) is unlikely to progress in a linear and incremental fashion, (c) will generate results that may not be amenable to measurement based on rationalist, Enlightenment understandings, and (d) can only be meaningfully understood in the context of the Third Horizon vision it is designed to serve.

The reality is that we can expect a "dilemma dance" rather than a simple linear model of incremental progress toward the Third Horizon. Transformational change does not happen in that step-by-step fashion. The evaluation framework itself will need to be an innovation and a strategic example to others.

SYSTEMS OF SUPPORT

Our experience suggests that what practitioners intent on transformative systems change need is processes, materials, prompts, advice, experience, and company to help them think through their next moves, their change initiatives, for themselves.

That is the main reason why this book has been written. It is accompanied by a deck of futures cards and a set of facilitation instructions described in detail in the Appendix. These form a simple set of resources to allow any group to use the frameworks and the content explored in this book to engage in a structured, time-limited, informed, and insightful conversation about the future and to feed that conversation forward into an innovation plan that is not just about improving the present.

The book also acts as a gateway to a wider set of resources, including those in the dedicated IFF Practice Centre at www.iffpraxis.com. These resources include:

- Simple tools and processes such as those outlined in previous chapters to help individuals and teams develop and pursue transformative proposals

- Transition tools to keep the process on track over time

- Resources focused on the producer competencies and on peer support that help with the human aspects of change

- A scanning function to highlight examples of inspiring practice in the present that suggest a Third Horizon vision is indeed achievable

As has been stressed many times throughout this book, transformative innovation is a social process, a process of social learning pursued in a human system. Hence the rule: no solo climbers. We need peer support, company on the journey. Equally, these materials and other resources will come to life only through shared experience and in community.

Part of the infrastructure of support therefore involves configuring the community of transformative innovators, a community of purpose with its eyes on aspirational change. And lying behind this community is another—of experienced practitioners, capable trainers and mentors, sources of guidance and advice.

The infrastructure that IFF has put in place is very much a private initiative, albeit based on substantial international support and experience. It is itself a transformative innovation, the attempt to establish a new pattern—a pattern that can be realized at any level from local to global and in any subject domain.

We hope that in time this initial effort to support transformative innovation in higher education will find a permanent home, a sustaining pattern of its own—ideally in a university or at least with a university as a prominent partner and with dedicated resources to enable it to support the sector as a whole.

This book, the facilitation resources in the Appendix, and our own group of dedicated advisors ready to support the practice of transformative innovation in higher education are the first small steps toward that goal. We hope these resources alone will be sufficient to start you on the same journey. Over time we will together establish in the landscape of higher education the patterns of renewal we need to encourage and support transformative change. By seeding and supporting pockets of future practice and resisting the siren calls of the First Horizon, we might at last start to shift our education systems, if not into the future, then at least into a fuller accommodation with the opportunities of an ever-flowing present.

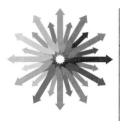

FACILITATING THREE HORIZONS FOR TRANSFORMATIVE INNOVATION

INTRODUCTION: THREE HORIZONS KIT FOR TRANSFORMATIVE INNOVATION

This book has introduced the Three Horizons framework to remind us to put ourselves in the picture when we think about the future (Chapter 1). It has outlined the complex factors, actors, and uncertainties shaping the future landscape for higher education (Chapter 2). It has suggested some tools and techniques for any institution to engage with this emerging landscape of change effectively in order to pursue a values-based, transformative pathway (Chapter 3). And it has outlined the supportive roles that strategy and policy can play in facilitating the transition to a new pattern of provision (Chapter 4).

Even so, it must be admitted that the process remains pretty complex—especially for schools and colleges already running at full capacity to face the day-to-day challenges of keeping things going. Which is why IFF has designed a simple Three Horizons Kit to enable any group to apply the frameworks explored in this book in the group's real-world circumstances (Figure A.1). The kit contains detailed facilitation instructions and a set of "futures cards" which should provide all the resources necessary for any group to engage in a structured, time-limited, well-informed, and insightful conversation about the future and to feed that conversation forward into an innovation plan that is not just about improving the present.

The process for such conversation is based on three sets of cards to prompt a strategic discussion about the present and the future. The statements on the cards are derived from the three scenarios for higher education described in Chapter 2, the research that informed them, and supplemental material from other relevant research projects. The cards are designed to provoke conversation about the changing world, about changing higher education policy and practice, and about the changing actors in the landscape, including young people themselves. Every statement on the cards is evidence-based, relating to something already happening, at some scale, somewhere in the world. This is a way of bringing current research and other knowledge quickly into the process—getting the future into the conversation about improvement in higher education. The card statements in all three categories are listed at the end of the appendix.

The kit and all accompanying resources are available at www.iffpraxis.com/transforming-higher-ed. In practice this book already contains, in greater detail and depth, much of

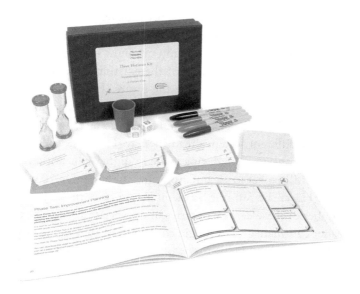

FIGURE A.1 **IFF's Three Horizons Kit for transformative innovation in higher education.**

the material included in the kit and the detailed facilitation instructions for hosting a Three Horizons conversation about transforming higher education are reproduced below. So readers are already well placed to get started. All that is missing are the futures cards used to seed the conversation: you will find these at the support website, available either as a physical deck (independent of the kit) or for use online.

The statements on the cards are used to prompt a conversation (hosted, e.g., by the college president or senior leader with senior staff) that is recorded, on sticky notes, on a Three Horizons chart against the two axes of pattern and time (see Figure 1.2). Senior students with experience in these conversations might themselves subsequently lead such a process by simply following the instructions below.

Each card statement stimulates a conversation about the nature of the Three Horizons landscape: Is what is referred to on the card happening already, or might it happen in the future? Is it a worrying sign of the existing system failing (H1) or a desirable feature for the future (H3)? Is it something that we or others are already taking into account in practice (H2) or that calls to mind inspirational examples of a radically different system already in play (H3 in the present)? Does it speak to an enduring value in higher education that we can still expect to see underpinning the system in 10 years' time (H1 in the future)? By facilitating a team in "playing" a number of these cards in a series of conversations, any group leader can manage a strategic conversation that in a couple of hours (or less) helps the team to populate its own Three Horizons landscape: concerns in the present, aspirations for the future, encouragement from present practice, and promising innovations already in play.

At this point groups will typically ask how to interpret the landscape they have discovered, and in particular how to incorporate the insights from their strategic conversation into practical implementation. So what?

Figure A.2 shows a second chart the group is then invited to complete, with a new set of instructions on how to process the initial Three Horizons conversation to draw out its implications for a program of innovation.

This second phase encourages the group to identify from its earlier conversation both a vision for the future (Box 1 in Figure A.2) and starting points in the present (Box 2). In other words, the group members develop the H3 ideal that they have identified and build on examples of that pattern they know of in the present (anywhere in the world). That implies a pathway to grow the Third Horizon. They can then draw up an innovation portfolio consisting of three kinds of action:

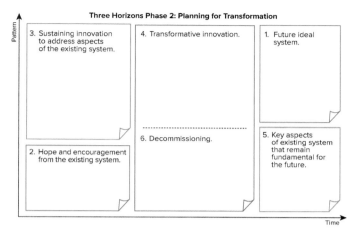

The second phase of the Three Horizons conversation. The process draws out the implications for an innovation strategy.

- Sustaining innovations required to address concerns about the existing system in order to keep it running (e.g., efficiency savings)

- Aspects of the existing system that have no place in their imagined ideal future and therefore need to be gradually "decommissioned"

- Transformative innovations that will pave the way for their H3 vision

This much we know is possible straight out of the box without skilled facilitation.

The kit also contains instructions, reproduced below, for the more detailed exercise involving the value tensions and navigational dilemmas outlined in Chapter 3. The process consists of first articulating the value tensions between a desirable Third Horizon and the business-as-usual First

Horizon, and then explaining how to work with the most critical tensions as navigational dilemmas to reveal promising innovation pathways for transformative action. This process is not quite as straightforward as the Phase Two chart in Figure A.2. But we have found that it makes for a better Phase Two conversation and a more robust innovation portfolio if it can be completed between Phase One and Phase Two.

The Three Horizons Kit and the Futures Cards are available from www.iffpraxis.com/transforming-higher-ed. With the material in this book and the facilitation instructions that follow, you already have most of what you need to get started.

FACILITATION INSTRUCTIONS

These instructions (which are also included in the physical kit) will allow you to put the frameworks, content, and other resources in this book to use in hosting workshops and other strategic conversations to explore your own creative and potentially transformative responses to the changing landscape in higher education.

The instructions are for a process that has two phases (mentioned in the discussion of the kit above):

- Phase One is an open conversation about the way things are today, trends in the world and in the domains of policy and emerging practice that might impact the way we do things at present, as well as the things we aspire to in the future. This conversation builds a shared Three Horizons map.

- Phase Two, probably run on a separate occasion and with a smaller group of people, is a conversation to translate the results of the first phase into an improvement plan, focusing on the things that need to change—innovation and decommissioning—in order to move toward the future you desire.

This process can be initiated by anyone within an organization who feels that a broad group conversation would be useful and is prepared to convene a group for that purpose.

The resources required are all contained in this book, including these instructions and:

- Templates for your Three Horizons map and for improvement planning

- A set of cards containing material relevant to the changing landscape of higher education

The cards are derived largely from the research and the scenarios described in Chapter 2. They provide a rapid way into a conversation where there is neither the time nor the resources to do detailed original background research.

You can convene a Three Horizons conversation without these cards, but the instructions that follow have been developed specifically to make use of them. As well as the physical card deck, you can also find an app at www.iffpraxis .com/transforming-higher-ed that will allow you to use the cards online (complete with shuffle and timer features) and to find alternative and updated card sets. You can also revise the cards there to suit your own circumstances.

If you are convening the conversation, you should *first familiarize yourself with the Three Horizons framework* as described in Chapter 1. You also need to think about how to record the conversation. Somebody needs to keep notes. It is possible for the convenor of the conversation to do this alone. But it might be easier to share the burden with another participant who can note significant points along the way—

particularly if there is somebody in the group who is known to be good at that. Anybody taking this role as note-taker also needs to have gained familiarity with the Three Horizons framework ahead of time.

Having sorted out these simple points of process management, you can call your chosen group together (the conversation will flow best with five to seven people including yourself) and get started using the instructions that follow.

PHASE ONE: OPEN CONVERSATION

As convenor of the conversation, you should let participants know:

1. Why you have brought them together

2. What the purpose of the conversation is

3. What you expect of them by way of contribution

4. How long it will take

5. What follow-up steps, if any, might flow from it

How you set up the conversation is critical to the way people will engage in it. What you want to encourage is a conversation that is open-ended, inclusive, and safe for people to participate in, and where participants feel they can share their real aspirations and concerns. It will help to reassure them that there is no right answer, that the conversation is not supposed to reach a conclusion at this stage, and that you (and any colleagues supporting you, e.g., a note-taker) will manage everything; their only role is to participate in the conversation as freely as possible.

Getting Started

The physical card deck and some kind of timing device (as you might find on your phone) provide the basic materials for the Phase One conversation. Alternatively, you can use the online deck and timer at www.iffpraxis.com/transforming-higher-ed. You will also need some good thick markers to write with (ideally red, blue, and green to match the Three Horizons), some sticky notes to record points made, and a Three Horizons chart on which to post them. You can download a chart for printing (poster size). Alternatively, if printing at that size is inconvenient, just use your markers to draw your own chart on a piece of flip-chart paper in landscape orientation using Figure 1.2 as a model.

We have found it easiest just to read out the following script in order to get started. It says all that needs to be said about the exercise and the Three Horizons framework—and informs the people in the room (including the convenor) about the process they are about to go through. Edit this as you see fit to suit your own purposes and context. It takes five minutes maximum (adding the optional "voices of the Three Horizons" exercise will add another five minutes).

Introductory Script

❝ Thank you for coming. This is a session to help us think about the future and what we might need to do as a result. There are three phases involved in the process overall:

- In Phase One we will have a conversation that encourages us to think about all the ways in which the world, our work, our lives, and the lives of our students are changing.

- In Phase Two, we make sense of that conversation and feed it into our future plans.

- In Phase Three we get into action: selecting actions from those plans and setting about putting them into practice.

These three phases have to happen in order. We are going to start today with Phase One. That is all we will be doing, and it will take about an hour.

Phase Two, which considers what all this means for our future plans, will happen on another occasion. So don't worry about solving all our problems in this session, or about where the conversation is going or what's going to happen next. There will be a "next," just not today.

It is important that we all contribute, because we are all involved and we all have different perspectives. This is not an examination. There are no right answers. It is a conversation that includes what we feel as individuals about how things are going and our own hopes and aspirations for the future. Nobody can say that those are wrong or that you shouldn't think or feel that way. So we don't try to convince each other and reach agreement on the points that come up—we value the variety of views.

Although we will take notes, you will not be called on later to justify what you say here. We want to keep this as natural and informal as possible.

The Three Horizons Chart

We'll record the conversation on a *Three Horizons chart*. This shows a simple way of representing a process of change over time. There is a dominant First Horizon (the red line) that equates to "business as usual," which gets less effective over time as the world changes. It slowly tails off into the background. [*Show it on the chart.*]

There is a Third Horizon (the green line) that is not very obvious at the moment; it is fringe activity, which can grow over time and come to replace the First Horizon and become the new business as usual.

Significantly, there is a space between these two, between the decline of the First Horizon and the growth of the Third, which rises and falls through a period of transition—this is the Second Horizon (the blue line). This represents a wave of innovations. Some of them work; some of them fail. Some of them help to improve our Horizon One systems; some help to support and grow the new Third Horizon.

You don't need to know anything more about the framework than that. I [*or a note-taker*] will record the conversation on the chart—which is helpful for the next phase of translating the conversation into improvement planning. **"**

Optional Exercise to Introduce the Three Horizons Concept as Distinctive "Voices" in the Conversation

What follows is the script for an exercise to practice the voices of the Three Horizons, as described in Figure 1.6. Our general experience is that people relate to these voices very easily and that doing this exercise brings the meaning of the Horizons alive in a quick and enjoyable way. This can be a useful warm-up if you have time and you judge that the group will play along.

Try saying the following:

" The way that this framework shows up in conversation is as three different voices relating to the Three Horizons. It might be useful to practice these before we get started.

Let's begin by thinking about what a typical H1 business-as-usual voice would say in a conversation about the future. This voice is the *voice of the manager* trying to keep the system going, a voice of concern (e.g., "There is no way we can go on providing the level of education our students expect if the money keeps falling"). Can you think of any other examples?

What might a typical H2 voice say? H2 is the *voice of the entrepreneur*, usually itching to get into action and to change things (e.g., "I heard they are using a new program in the University of X that automatically tracks learning outcomes. Why can't we do that?"). Any other examples?

Then there is the H3 voice. This is the most difficult, the one that is least often heard or expressed in the conversation because it is personal and values-based and often written off as irrelevant. H3 is the *voice of the visionary*, the voice of aspiration and hope (e.g., "Have we forgotten that this was never about data and test scores and jobs—that it is about educating people for life?"). Any examples of this voice?

> In recording the conversation I will be listening for all three voices. I hope everyone will feel able to express them all—including the Third Horizon voice, which is rarely heard in a professional context. **"**

It might also be useful preparation to hand out copies of Figure 1.6 of the Horizon voices—this helps people recognize the typical interactions that happen between them.

The Cards

" The deck of cards works to prompt the conversation, to both stimulate and challenge us. The cards fall into three suits: changing world, changing higher education policy, and changing young people. Some of the statements on the cards are quite provocative. Some you may not agree with. But they are all based on evidence and rooted in reality.

The *way the game is played* is very simple. For each round, one of us takes a turn to select a card at random from the deck. [*You might like to take a card at this point to act as an illustration.*]

First the person who picked the card will read it aloud so that everyone knows what it says and we can check that people understand what it means. Then whoever has picked the card starts a conversation about the issue on the card by saying what it means to him or her. Try answering three questions about it:

- Is this happening already or likely to happen in the future—is there a trend under way that is growing stronger over time?

- Is it a good thing or a bad thing, and who is it that thinks so—what are people doing about it, and can we see what they are doing somewhere in the world?

- Are we already taking it into account in our own work, or is it something we need to think about for the future? Or is it irrelevant?

We will use a sand timer (*this is what is used in the physical kit—alternatively use the timer on your phone or built into the online app: three minutes a round is about right*) to move the conversation along. When the time is up, that is a signal to move to the next player— although we might want to extend some conversations if they are getting interesting. But if the timer has run out, participants can draw attention to that if they want to move on. So don't worry if the conversation seems to be getting bogged down on an issue, or straying off track, or whatever—it will not stay that way for long.

Lastly, the deck also contains three *jokers*. These are blank cards. If you draw the joker, it means you can introduce anything you like into the conversation— including commenting on the way things are going in the session generally.

Any questions?

Then we'll begin. [*Shuffle the deck of cards one more time and hand them to the player on your left to pick one at random.*]**"**

Managing the Conversation

The role of the convenor, once the conversation is under way, is to keep it moving and support everyone's involvement. You are helping each member of the group to contribute to a shared understanding of the landscape of change and to bring into play the person's own ambitions and vision for the topic under discussion.

There is a style to this type of work that may be unfamiliar, as it lies somewhere between a typical discussion in which you try to agree on something and a brainstorming session where you just want to get lots of ideas out.

In this process, less is more—you want around 30 to 40 well-captured points, not a blizzard of sticky notes—one or two points for each card. The note-taker's job is to capture in a few words a point from the conversation that has been understood by everyone and to place the note on the map so everyone can see where it has been recorded.

Each point just needs to be *understood* by everyone, not agreed. There is a value in a diversity of views. This is what will build up a rich shared map among all the participants. Try to capture points in the words with which they were made—then people feel heard, and it makes it easy to move on to the next contribution.

Keeping a steady pace of well-captured points builds a strong shared understanding that will carry forward into Phase Two. The map is building up a shared space for everyone's contribution to be seen together.

When people first pick a card, you may need to prompt them so they understand how to respond. The first thing to check is whether everyone understands what the card says. Then if an individual is stumped, you can work through the three questions repeated here from above (it can be helpful to write short versions of them on a flip chart as a reminder):

- Is this happening already or likely to happen in the future—is there a trend under way that is growing stronger over time?

- Is it a good thing or a bad thing, and who is it that thinks so—what are people doing about it, and can we see what they are doing somewhere in the world?

- Are we already taking it into account in our own work, or is it something we need to think about for the future? Or is it irrelevant?

Note that it is this final question that steers the conversation into the future for your organization and your concerns and the sort of responses that might be needed—incremental or transformative.

Use a timer to help keep the conversation flowing. The initial rounds might take a little longer while people get the hang of things. And you will know when the conversation is getting interesting and it would pay to linger. The ping of the timer is a good signal you can use to move on to a new card.

Make sure you also get a turn to pick a card and initiate a round of conversation (if you are taking the notes, pass on that role to someone else for this round).

You will probably feel the point where the session wants to draw naturally to a close. The simple way of putting this is to say that you should continue until the time allotted, the cards, or the participants are exhausted. This will vary from group to group but is likely to be around an hour. Smaller groups (e.g., three people) might be quicker. As noted above, getting around 30 to 40 points (1 or 2 per card) that have been carefully captured and heard by everyone will build a good map.

The ideal is to schedule a 90-minute session for six people—which allows everyone to have a good chance to play and also some time at the end for overall reflections on the conversation.

Note-Taking

It is important that the convenor or a note-taker records significant points from the discussion on sticky notes and places them on the Three Horizons map. It is enough to capture just one or two key points from the discussion of each card.

Ideally you should use three good, thick, colored markers to represent the Three Horizons: H1 (red), H2 (blue), and H3 (green).

When a point is made, check your understanding of which Horizon it belongs in and use the right color marker to write it down:

First Horizon (Red)

- Expressions of worry or concern; ways in which the First Horizon pattern is failing to respond to change.

- Statements about visible signs of stress or failure in the current pattern that suggest a failure to adapt well to change.

Second Horizon (Blue)

- Innovations appearing that respond to this change and that are trying to shift the First Horizon pattern; these are likely to be real people doing real things or ideas that are being actively discussed even if not yet introduced.

Third Horizon (Green)

- Significant changes in culture or society—the surrounding landscape—that may emerge strongly in the future and demand a transformative response or open up new fields of innovation.

- Visions, aspirations, dreams that are being put forward which relate either to the opportunities in a changing culture or to the sense that the First Horizon pattern has had its day and something radically different is needed. These aspirations might be good or bad, other people's or our own.

- Pockets of the future in the present—real examples of inspirational practice at the margin of today's mainstream that inspire and encourage the speaker to believe another world is possible.

Note that you will also get a clue about whether points relate to H1, H2, or H3 from the tone of voice of the speaker. Does the person sound like a concerned manager (First Horizon, red), an excited or frustrated entrepreneur (Second Horizon, blue), or an inspired and emotionally moved visionary (Third Horizon, green)?

Once you have the color coding, the next question is where on the chart to place the note. Place each one, as you write it, under the peak of its respective Horizon: the First Horizon (red) on the left, Second Horizon (blue) in the middle, and Third Horizon (green) on the right.

After this you might then add a sense of *timing* within the horizons: well-established trends or facts to the left of the timeline, emerging factors further to the right. But this is not essential and should not distract you from what is already quite a demanding task of keeping track of the conversation.

The color coding should make it easier to start to see three emerging stories—about the troubles with the First Horizon and its slow decline (red), about a wave of innovations and entrepreneurial activity (blue), and about inspirational practice in the present that might yet grow to realize an aspirational vision for the future (green).

The aim of the session overall is to populate the Three Horizons landscape described by the participants—to generate a Three Horizons map.

PHASE TWO: IMPROVEMENT PLANNING

Where Phase One is focused on an open conversation that links the present (the First Horizon) and the future (the Third Horizon) through a process of transition (the Second Horizon), Phase Two involves applying the deeper understanding gained from the discussion to the nuts and bolts of improvement planning and action.

It is best to run Phase Two on another occasion (not too long after the original conversation) and probably with a smaller group responsible for planning and decision making.

The challenge of Phase Two is to develop a clear view of the change and innovation required, in both the short and the longer term. You should use your Third Horizon vision as the goal to strive toward, and your discussion around the current position (H1) and your Second Horizon ideas as guides for your innovation planning.

The chart for Phase Two has six boxes and is shown in Figure A.2. You can download this chart for printing (at poster size) from www.iffpraxis.com/transforming-higher-ed. Alternatively you can draw your own on a piece of landscape-oriented flip-chart paper, numbering the boxes as shown.

You can use the chart to go through the process below. Alternatively, if you have the time and the inclination and some confidence in facilitating the conversation, there is a rather more advanced process outlined later in this appendix that picks up on the material in Chapter 3 of this book about value tensions and the need to navigate dilemmas on the journey between the First and Third Horizon. If that feels like a facilitation too far, you will find that filling in the six-box chart (Figure A.2) following the process below is quite satisfactory and certainly enough to identify transformative intentions and people in the room willing to commit some energy to them.

Simple Process: Filling in the Six Boxes

Review Current Concerns

As a starting point, take a look at the sticky notes from your Phase One discussions about the features of the existing system, the First Horizon, that are causing you concern. Summarize these into a series of bullet points or headlines reflecting a common understanding among your group. You may want first to cluster the sticky notes into groups of points that are related. You can do this either in conversation or in silence as a group. This is a good way to make better sense of a collection of points. No more than seven points per cluster is a good rule of thumb, so that they don't all just end up in one large clump. These are the main elements of the existing system that your plans need to address. Keep this list in front of you as you go through the next steps.

Now turn to the Phase Two chart and in the following order begin to transcribe the issues and actions recorded on your sticky notes on to this second chart. You might simply transfer some sticky notes, cluster some together under a fresh heading, or write and record directly on to the chart.

Completing the Boxes in Order

Complete Box 1

Take a look at the sticky notes from your conversation about the aspirations you expressed for a new, desirable system in the Third Horizon. Just as you did for the First Horizon above, summarize these aspirations into a series of bullet points or headlines in Box 1.

This step may be quite testing. Our visionary aspirations are usually based on an implicit set of values that might not be held in common by all those involved in the conversation. If elements of your aspirations seem incompatible within your team, then you may need a deeper discussion about values in order to clarify a shared vision of the future. The advanced process outlined in the Pathways to the Third Horizon section below might help.

Complete Box 2

Having discussed a desirable future, it should be possible to identify aspects of that future happening already or features of current practice that can be built upon. You can now summarize, as a set of bullet points in Box 2, the examples of radical practice that you have already discussed and recorded on your sticky notes. Add to them if you need to. Consider those aspects of current practice, either in your own setting or anywhere else in the world, that give you hope and encouragement that the future you desire is indeed achievable.

Complete Boxes 3 and 4

Take a look again at the list of concerns about the existing system that you expressed at the start of this exercise (in the "Review Current Concerns" section above). Consider what you have said about your desirable future (you have listed headlines in Box 1) and some of the things already happening that can encourage you to undertake the journey (you have listed these in Box 2). You are now ready to tackle the challenge of designing an innovation strategy that will both improve the existing system and help you make the transition to something even better.

(Optional: Cut to advanced process at this point.)

In completing these next two boxes, you need to identify, first, the *sustaining innovations* that will help keep the system running and address immediate concerns and, second, the *transformative innovations* that will support the journey toward your longer-term aspirations. You need both.

Sifting the actions and innovations in this way is likely to be a novel process for most people, but it is one of the advantages that the Three Horizons approach offers: now you can attempt the twin-track innovation process of "redesigning the plane while flying it."

Try the following sequence:

- Review what you recorded on your sticky notes in the middle Second Horizon zone on the Three Horizons chart. Note down the transformative and sustaining innovations that you have already recorded on your sticky notes and prioritize them by selecting those that you think have a part to play in your future and that will make a difference. Place them in Boxes 3 and 4: Box 3 for sustaining innovations, Box 4 for transformative innovations.

- Add to the list from your own experience. What are the innovations that are in play in your setting, in current policy, in your wider experience? Note that the transformative innovations will likely come from those stories of practice that particularly energize, excite, or inspire you.

Some sustaining innovations can be tweaked to give them a greater focus on your Third Horizon vision. See whether any of the sustaining innovations you have noted could be modified to become transformative.

Complete Box 5

This is the box in which you include the essential, foundational aspects of the existing system that you will want to maintain in the future.

Do not spend too long on this stage; it is a preparation for the final step (below). But it can help you to see that the First Horizon is not "wrong." Significant change needs to occur over time—but through intelligent transformation, not revolution.

Complete Box 6

As well as introducing new actions and innovations, your innovation strategy must also decommission aspects of current practice that have no place in your desired future or are low impact in the present. This is challenging, because there are many things we do or support as professionals or as concerned citizens that we are reluctant to give up, but we must. So in this box you should put any ideas for clearing the way, that is, aspects of present practice that could be discontinued to make way for the new.

This completes the Phase Two chart. Skip to the final section of this Appendix, "Implementing Transformative Innovation," for some concluding thoughts on how to get into action: support for implementation.

ADVANCED PROCESS:
PATHWAYS TO THE THIRD HORIZON

Transformative innovation that shifts the system toward a desired future is not easy. You are likely to find that a program of "sustaining innovation" is easier to deliver. For that reason, such a program can easily squeeze out your longer-term aspirations.

As described in Chapter 3, it is usually the case that the dominant First Horizon pattern today is configured around some very stable and familiar structures—such as schools, hospitals, prisons, universities, etc. As those structures begin to feel as if they are no longer fit for purpose, they are likely to give way to other structures, other patterns. But we may still want to preserve some of the *values* that typically underpin such First Horizon structures: managerial values like efficiency, reliability, safety, and so on.

On the other hand, people are likely to aspire to a different Third Horizon pattern, partly because the First Horizon structures we have developed to embody these managerial vaues now seem to suppress other values: our structures have become large and mechanistic, squeezing out the human dimension, for example. So the growth of the Third Horizon pattern is a move in the opposite direction, from values expressed in the margins in the present to structures embodying those values as central in the future.

One of the things that makes the shift from an H1 pattern to an H3 pattern so difficult to realize in practice is the fact that in moving toward H3, we are typically moving against values embodied in the present system that we are reluctant to give up.

Value Tensions

It can be very helpful to identify these value tensions so as to be able to work skillfully with them. The chart in Figure A.3 helps with this process. You can download it for printing (at poster size) from www.iffpraxis.com/transforming-higher-ed. Alternatively you can draw your own on a piece of flip-chart paper used in landscape format.

You will already have followed the first steps from the Phase Two process described in previous pages. Thus you will have a good feel for concerns relating to the current First Horizon pattern and a short summary of it from your Phase One discussion. You will also have a good feel for the Third Horizon pattern and a short summary of it.

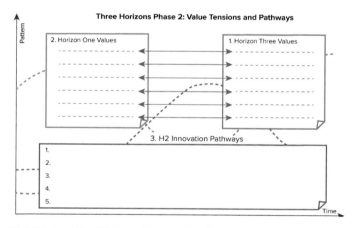

FIGURE A.3 **Identifying value tensions between the First and Third Horizons and the promising Second Horizon innovation pathways that might provide a feasible route between them honoring both sets of values.**

With these descriptions in mind, you are now ready to work with the Value Tensions and Pathways chart (Figure A.3), as follows:

1. Take a look at the Third Horizon pattern and search for the values that underpin it. What is it that this pattern values? When you have identified a value, place it on the chart in Box 1.

2. Now identify a corresponding value underpinning the First Horizon pattern with which it is in tension. Write that in Box 2.

Typical examples might be the Horizon Three pattern placing a value on freedom and autonomy to experiment in tension with Horizon One valuing reliable and repeatable bureaucratic processes. Or Horizon Three valuing subjective experience in tension with a Horizon One valuing objective evidence.

The more polarized these pairs of values are, the more powerful the process will be. So focus on making each one as strong as possible—when you've filled in both sides of the tension, you may want to reword what you wrote in order to bring out the tension more clearly.

Repeat this until you have no more than six pairs of values. If you find yourself wanting more than this, then try to replace a less important H3 value with a more important one. If you have too many, the process becomes less focused and effective.

The most important thing is to remember that the First Horizon value is something valuable. It is all too easy to fall into describing H1 in negative terms. But what we are looking for is something that you can see as a *good thing* in the present system, even if it is reducing the room for another good thing you would like to see more of in the Third Horizon.

A good way to make sure the tension is really explored is to divide the group into two teams representing the First and Third Horizon values and have them make the case against each other. This makes the process more playful and creative and helps to point up the tension while keeping both sides positive.

Dilemmas

Having identified the significant value tensions in the landscape, you next need to work out how to navigate an innovation pathway between them. The requirement in these circumstances is not just to make a choice between one value and the other but to treat them as a dilemma in which the ideal is a marriage of both—for example, reliability *and* experiment (to use the examples above), or action based on evidence *and* experience.

The characteristic of a dilemma is precisely that it tugs us between two positive values where a simple choice is inadequate. If we place the values in tension not at different ends of a spectrum but at right angles, we create a "dilemma space" with a sweet spot in which we can combine the best of *both* values—where we can have our cake and eat it.

The smart H2+ innovation pathway will be leading toward the resolution of the dilemma; we will consciously be steering a path between the two poles and using the tension between them as a source of propulsion, a motive force to determine the direction of travel toward the creative resolution in the Third Horizon. It is like propelling a sailboat by working with the often competing forces of the wind and the waves.

As described in more detail earlier (see the section, "Identifying Navigational Dilemmas") there are five possible outcomes in managing a dilemma in this way. To work through the critical dilemmas that arise from a Three Horizons conversation, it is helpful to divide the dilemma space into these five zones. You can use Figure A.4 to work with each value tension in turn.

You can download this chart for printing (at poster size) from www.iffpraxis.com/transforming-higher-ed. Alternatively you can draw your own on a piece of flip-chart paper, numbering the boxes as shown.

Take the value tension and place the H1 and H3 values on the two axes of the chart as shown in Figure A.4. Then we can perform the following step-by-step process (first introduced in Chapter 3), working through the zones in order and capturing the thoughts of the group on sticky notes in each zone:

- **Zone 1.** State what is essential from this perspective. What would we do if we favored this perspective?

- **Zone 2.** State what is essential from this perspective. What would we do if we favored this perspective?

- **Zone 3.** What are the typical activities that arise from a compromise between the two values? How is the tension between them typically managed in practice?

- **Zone 4.** Where are the values in conflict? What are the (unresolved) arguments that currently take place between them?

- **Zone 5.** Seek creative resolution. What can the Zone 1 value offer the Zone 2 value without loss of integrity, and vice versa?

Three Horizons Phase 2: Navigational Dilemmas

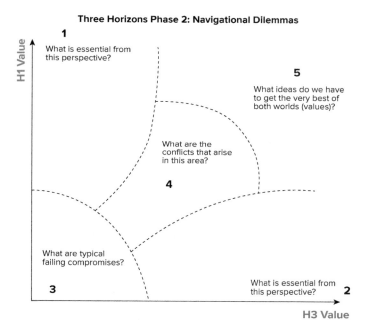

Sequence

1. State what is essential from the perspective of the H1 value.
2. State what is essential from the perspective of the H3 value.
3. Identify some of the typical compromises that sweep things under the carpet.
4. Characterize the tensions that can break out into conflicts between these two values.
5. Seek creative resolution.
   a. What can the H1 value offer the H3 value without compromise?
   b. What can the H3 value offer the H1 value without compromise?
   c. Generate new ideas using the creative 1 + 1 = 3 principle: if you put the ideas side by side, what is implied between them?

FIGURE A.4 **Working with the five zones in a dilemma space to seek creative resolution.** (© *International Futures Forum, 2009*)

Finally, take all the resolution ideas in Zone 5 and ask what it is that they have in common. This will reveal the innovation pathway—the innovation route you need to take to reach this pattern of resolution.

Write your innovation pathway for this pair of values into Box 3 on the "Value Tensions and Pathways" chart in Figure A.3.

Repeat this process for each of the H1–H3 value tensions.

Implementing Transformative Innovation

You may now return to your original Three Horizons map and put some flesh on the bones of each innovation pathway, populating it with ideas for transformative innovation.

For each innovation pathway, consider these questions:

- What actions can you initiate (these can be small scale) to start exploring the innovation pathway? These actions are the seeds of transformative innovation.

- Are there suitable H2+ innovations already recorded in the Second Horizon (blue) sticky notes from your original conversation? Do the Third Horizon (green) examples of hope, encouragement, and inspiration in the present give you any ideas?

- How do you want to relate to these examples—competitors, collaborators, inspiration, learning partners? Look again at Figure 1.6 showing how the different voices of the Three Horizons speak about each other for some possible prompts.

You are looking for acorns at this stage, not oak trees. This should make initiating radical innovation feel less daunting.

Think about actions that might satisfy the following criteria:

- Is small in scale

- Inspires at least two or three members of staff willing to support one another in giving it a go (i.e., avoid "solo climbers")

- Releases resources from the First Horizon system and directs them toward the Third Horizon (i.e., does not require large, additional, up-front investment)

- Provides a management structure—at the very least a small group of people committed to working together, a "creative integrity"—and measures that allow the Third Horizon to grow alongside the First with distinct and appropriate measures for its success

- Authentically illustrates the big picture developed in the earlier open conversation by fitting a transition pathway toward your Third Horizon vision rather than simply improving the present system

- Is viral in nature in that others will adopt these changes because they work and not because they are imposed in a top-down manner

This advanced process will provide you with a more sophisticated portfolio of transformative innovations—Box 4 in the Phase Two chart (Figure A.2). For completeness it is also worth finally visiting Boxes 5 and 6 so as not to miss the aspects of the First Horizon pattern that need to be maintained through the transition and those that need to be decommissioned in order to make space, and free up resources, for the new.

Support for Implementation

You should by now have developed, from the initial open conversation in Phase One, the broad outlines of a plan for improvement and transformative innovation in Phase Two.

Thereafter, making headway in Phase Three, getting into action, will require you and your colleagues, or at least the pioneers among you, to be courageous in taking the first steps into the unknown toward your envisaged Third Horizon. Equally, you will need to do so with discipline and with a plan that is rooted in the challenges of the real world.

There is a range of conversational tools and frameworks available to help. IFF uses those developed by our colleague Jim Ewing of Executive Arts. These can be accessed via the IFF Practice Centre.

There you will also find other resources, including skilled facilitators and advisors, to support you in making improvements in practice. You may also want to sign up on IFF's Transformative Innovation Network where you can connect with others, in your field and in other domains, who are actively working to shift the patterns in which they work toward an aspirational, viable, and fulfilling Third Horizon. Visit www.iffpraxis.com to get started.

FUTURES CARDS

These statements, printed as a deck of cards, help to stimulate the conversation about transforming higher education, introducing current research and other knowledge quickly into the process. The cards are available at www.iffpraxis.com/transforming-higher-ed, both as a physical deck and for use online.

Changing Higher Education

- While higher education provides knowledge, young people seek wisdom elsewhere.

- Diminishing returns on investment in existing forms of education become apparent.

- Written examination of individual performance is the gold standard.

- Higher education is charged with preparing young people for jobs that don't yet exist.

- The identification and cultivation of emotional competencies is an integral element in all higher education.

- Technology enables education to be an industrialized, standardized, and accessible product.

- Institutional transparency is the universal standard.

- Higher education is less and less affordable and more and more irrelevant.

- Schools offer standardized programs, but young people want experience in the world.

- Learning across the life span is based on age-specific requirements, pedagogy, and assessment.

- In the new knowledge ecosystem, we need educators, but we don't need universities.

- Employers look for "signals" of qualification/competence other than degrees.

- Students "roll their own" degree courses between different modules and institutions.

- Education is a global business dominated by a few powerful providers.

- Education for the twenty-first century shifts emphasis from disciplinary to transdisciplinary knowledge.

- The core mission of education is dominated by the language of business and economics.

- College provides "safe spaces" for academic risk taking and for development of student resilience.

- Education is increasingly framed as a personal investment in "the start-up of you."

- Students demand that colleges deliver what is needed for career readiness and career agility.

- Evolving technology offers the holy grail of personalized, guided instruction for all students.

- Spaces for experiential learning are greatly enhanced by virtual and augmented reality.

- Higher education is "texting while driving"—adopting new technologies with little regard for wider consequences.

- Majors not of interest to corporate sponsors are dropped, relegating liberal arts courses to second division.

- Faculty terms of employment move closer to other workers, with tenure a rarity outside research institutions.

Changing Young People

- The "market of one" becomes the norm, e.g., mass media to "my media."

- "The network is the qualification"—it's not what you know but whom you know.

- Anxiety, depression, and mental distress increase in the college population.

- Young people search for meaning in a portfolio of beliefs.

- Knowledge is no longer seen as a product to deliver or acquire but an ecosystem to navigate, participate in, and create.

- The balance between lifetime earnings and employment chances and the debt burdens of higher education no longer make sense to young people.

- The peer-to-peer character of new technology fosters a natural culture of collaboration and coproduction.

- A gaming paradigm of challenge, fun, and immersion is becoming a mainstream pedagogy.

- Youth groups enabled by social networking technologies coordinate engaged activism across many issues.

- Many young people are left struggling to develop the cognitive and emotional entry requirements for a global culture.

- Complex, fluid, multiple identities are common and more lightly held.

- Global citizenship is a meaningful concept for young people.

- Young people find certainty in uncertain times through identifying with fundamentalisms.

- Youth unemployment creates a lost generation.

- Standards are in decline: students are no longer likely to be as educated as their parents.

- The number of college students worldwide is increasing fast—it has tripled since 2000.

- Students expect education to be something that they help design, not something that just happens to them.

- Graduates seek a sense of purpose and civic engagement beyond making money.

- Students brought up in a grade-focused culture see failure not as a learning experience but as a personal rebuke.

- The fundamental problem in higher education is not the availability of content but the motivation to engage with it.

Changing World

- The boundaries between school, community, workplace, college, and university are blurred.

- Most people never retire.

- There are no more jobs for life: today's learners will have at least 15 different jobs before they turn 40.

- The majority of young people will live to see the twenty-second century.

- Ethical issues move center stage in public discourse.

- The context for successful learning and effective contribution is global.

- Cheap, plentiful energy comes to an end.

- Rising stress and distress in an "always on," 24/7 culture.

- Happiness and well-being are seen as more important than GDP growth.

- Socioeconomic inequalities increase and deepen.

- Social media, social networking, and citizen journalism undermine established institutions of authority and power.

- China has a higher number of English speakers than any other country in the world.

- Increasing migration leads to ever greater cultural and religious diversity within nations.

- The operating context for the world of work is now volatile, uncertain, complex and ambiguous (VUCA).

- Graduates need to be problem finders, not just problem solvers.

- Jobs are temporary: they are short-term "gigs" or longer-term "tours of duty" at best.

- Up to 50% of college graduates are underemployed, working in jobs that don't require graduate-level education.

- Having a degree is now about beating less educated workers to the barista and clerical jobs.

- Corporations' choice of higher education partners for employee is programs now more influential than formal accreditation.

INDEX

ABOUT THE AUTHORS

Graham Leicester is a founder and director of International Futures Forum (IFF). He previously ran Scotland's leading think tank, the Scottish Council Foundation, founded in 1997. From 1984 to1995 he served as a diplomat in Her Majesty's Diplomatic Service, specializing in China (he speaks Mandarin Chinese) and the EU. Between 1995 and 1997 he was senior research fellow with the Constitution Unit at University College London. He has also worked as a freelance professional cellist, including with the BBC Concert Orchestra. He has strong interests in governance, systems change, education, and healthcare. His most recent publications include *Transformative Innovation in Education: A Playbook for Pragmatic Visionaries, Dancing at the Edge: Competence, Culture and Organisation in the 21st Century* (with Maureen O'Hara), and *Transformative Innovation: A Guide to Practice and Policy* (all with Triarchy Press).

Bill Sharpe is a futures practitioner and independent researcher in science, technology, and society. He was a research lab director at Hewlett Packard Laboratories where he led research into everyday applications of technology and introduced scenario methods to HP to support long-range research and innovation. Since leaving HP, he has specialized in science, technology, and policy studies for business strategy and public policy foresight. With a background in psychology, he is particularly interested in drawing on leading-edge research in cognition and systems thinking to find new ways of tackling complex problems. He is a member of International Futures Forum and author of *Economies of Life: Patterns of Health and Wealth* and *Three Horizons: The Patterning of Hope* (both with Triarchy Press).

To learn more, visit www.iffpraxis.com.